GOING BEYOND WORDS

The Art and Practice of Visual Thinking

KATHY MASON

ZEPHYR PRESS

3316 North Chapel Avenue
Tucson, AZ 85716-1416
P.O. Box 13448
Tucson, AZ 85732-3448
(602) 322-5090
FAX (602) 323-9402

ZEPHYR PRESS
Tucson, Arizona

Going Beyond Words
Grades 4 – 8
©1989 Kathy Mason
©1991 Zephyr Press, Tucson, Arizona
ISBN 0–913705–61–6

This book was edited by Mary Colgan McNamara, The inside illustrations are the work of Kathy Price. "The Blindman" by May Swenson is reprinted by permission of the author, copyright ©1965 by May Swenson.

Specific terminology used to explain each step of the eight-part 4MAT model in Part II is from Bernice McCarthy's *4MAT Learning Style System.*

*This book is dedicated
to my children,
Brandon and Lindsay.*

*Through their vision
I am reminded that before words,
Images are.*

acknowledgements

I would like to thank the following people for their help with various aspects of the book:

My mother, an unusually creative classroom teacher, understood the importance of integrating art activities throughout the curriculum. Students in her fifth grade classroom stitched a quilt every year. They made candles, built replicas of early forts, and expressed themselves throughout the year with visual arts activities. My mother's creative spirit has strongly influenced my own use of visual arts as a way to know.

To create the units throughout this book, I used the 4MAT Learning Style System of Dr. Bernice McCarthy, a well-known leader in the field of learning style/brain dominance research. As you travel around the wheels in line, shape, color, texture, and freehand drawing, as well as the wheels of discovery, know that you are participating in a cycle designed to reach the individual needs of every learning style. The 4MAT system will always be the foundations of any curriculum I write or teach because it honors every learner.

In all truthfulness, I do not know if this book would have been published without the help of my editor and friend, Mary Colgan McNamara. After reading the initial manuscript, she began to ask questions, the kind of insightful questions that send an author back to the typewriter. I have explored and expanded many parts of *Going Beyond Words* due to Mary's inspiration.

When I need someone to extend my own understanding of visual thinking or field test a new strategy, I visit Kathy Carless, a classroom teacher who has always emphasized visual thinking strategies in her classroom. She and her students have been an invaluable resource.

A special thank you to Kathy Price for the magnificent illustrations which appear throughout *Going Beyond Words*.

My own students have provided original drawings and poetry. They did a wonderful job of "acting natural" whenever the photographer wanted to take a picture.

The following teachers from Visalia Unified School District have submitted instructional units that appear in Part III. Like the visual arts wheels, these units were created using Bernice McCarthy's 4MAT System.

Dinosaurs — Susi Binova
Wind — Kathy Mason
Beginning Reading—The Sound of R — Kathy Howerton, Coordinator, Primary
    Education
Pioneers on the Oregon Trail — Ted Mason
Fairy Tale Lore — Vicki Black
Christopher Columbus — Kathy Mason
Right Angles — Kathy Carless
The Renaissance — Ron Howard
Camera Eye Descriptions — Judy Lucas
The Portrait of a President — Kathy Mason
Beowulf — Judy Lucas
Cell Design — Kathy Falconer

contents . . .

a sheet of large
white drawing paper

I am in elementary school. It is the last hour of the day on Friday afternoon and we are having art. My teacher has provided every student with a sheet of 12x18 white drawing paper. "Take out your crayons and draw a picture," she says. We are given some suggestions but the teacher makes it clear that the choice is ours. At first I am calm, certain that an idea will come. But as the minutes escape, I begin to panic. Everyone else seems to be absorbed in drawing. Am I the only one who isn't drawing something? I have always enjoyed writing stories. However, I would rather take a history test than draw a picture. Why? Because I'm not an artistic sort of person. Oh no. . . the period is almost over. My paper, like my mind, is blank. The teacher will wonder. . . Should I simply draw a few quick mountains, add some clouds, and stick a sun up in the corner? It's not something I'd want to share with anyone but at least I'll be done.

visual thinking and visual art — a vital connection

T he arts are neglected because they are based on perception, and perception is disdained because it is not assumed to involve thought. In fact, educators and administrators cannot justify giving the arts an important position in the curriculum unless they understand that the arts are the most powerful means of strengthening the perceptual component without which productive thinking is impossible in every field of academic study.

What is most needed is not more aesthetics or more esoteric manuals of art education but a convincing case made for visual thinking quite in general. Once we understand in theory we might try to heal in practice the unwholesome split which cripples the training of reasoning power.

Rudolf Arnheim
Visual Thinking

visual atrophy

During elementary and junior high school, I had many other uncomfortable experiences with large white drawing paper. In 4th grade I was given a low mark on my report card in art. The teacher wrote that I lacked creativity and motivation during art period. This comment disturbed me a great deal and I came to the conclusion that it would be best to leave art to those with talent. For many years that is just what I did.

Later it became clear that I was not the only person on this planet who felt ill at ease with art. Many if not most of the classroom teachers I meet are insecure about their ability to draw and provide art instruction in the classroom. As one 5th grade teacher told me, "When I was a student, we spent the entire day studying academic subjects so that we would be able to do well in college. I don't think anyone felt that learning how to draw or take part in art activities would help us be successful as adults. Also, I'm not sure that any of my teachers ever learned how to draw when they were in school." This statement brings to the surface two important questions. Is it necessary for every student to learn how to draw? And, how important is art instruction in a child's education?

While reading *Experiences In Visual Thinking* by Robert McKim, I encountered the term visual atrophy.[1] These two words became a neon sign in my mind. As a veteran classroom teacher, I have observed a kind of visual atrophy which occurs when students are provided with a one-sided education in the 3 R's. Taught always to name what they see, many students attach a label to the visual stimulus before they really see it. For example, word-dependent learners rarely see trees in all their many shades of green. They fail to notice the shape of a limb and the feel of the bark. Nor do they observe the complex relationship of the trunk, bark, limb, twig, and leaf. When asked to draw a tree, students whose visual perception has atrophied struggle unsuccessfully to draw a lifelike tree or instead choose to simply draw a roundish green circle with a brown stick for a trunk. Their inability to draw one of the most common life forms on our planet is a symptom of an educational system that focuses almost entirely on secondhand reality encoded in words and numbers.

I am certain that one major reason many educators view art instruction as a frill is because they are not aware that thinking can occur in other than verbal and mathematical modes. To better understand the importance of visual modes of thought, it is worth considering two notable scientific discoveries, both of which are cited in McKim's book.

Penicillin. Sir Alexander Flemming had been working with some plates of staphylococci. After opening the plates several times they became contaminated. He observed that staphylococci around one particular colony had died. This observation by itself was not particularly remarkable since it had long been known that some bacteria interfere with the growth of others. Flemming, however, went on to discover penicillin. He saw the possible significance of what had occurred because he possessed an ability to see things from a new, fresh perspective. He didn't look and then sit down to think, he used his active eyes and mind together.

The Structure of the DNA Molecule Nobel Laureate James Watson and his colleagues visualized the structure of the DNA molecule by building a large three dimensional molecule. In The Double Helix, Watson provides a fascinating account of the way in which the structure of the DNA molecule was discovered. He writes: "Only a little encouragement was needed to get the final soldering accomplished in the next couple of hours. The brightly shining metal plates were then immediately used to make a model in which for the first time all the DNA components were present. In about an hour I had arranged the atoms in positions which satisfied both the X-ray data and the laws of stereo chemistry. The resulting helix was right-handed with the two chains running in opposite directions."[2]

Inner imagery of the mind's eye plays an important role in the thought processes of many creative people. For example, Nikola Tesla whose inventions included the fluorescent light and the A-C generator "could project before his eyes a picture complete in every detail, of every part of a machine. These pictures were more vivid than any blueprint." In fact, Tesla's mental imagery was so highly developed that he was able to build his complex inventions without drawings.

Albert Einstein, in a famous letter written to Jacques Hadamard, relates the vital role of inner imagery in his own extremely abstract thinking: "The words or language, as they are written and spoken, do not seem to play any role in my mechanism of thought. The psychical entities which seem to serve as elements in thought are certain signs and more or less clear images which can be voluntarily reproduced and combined. . . Conventional words or other signs have been sought for laboriously in a second stage, when the above mentioned associative play is sufficiently established and can be reproduced at will."[3]

In a typical classroom, students spend most of their day acquiring reading, writing, and math skills that detach them from firsthand experience. Yet sensory modes of thought, particularly the visual, are at the very heart of thinking. I became especially aware of this dilemma when students attempted to do simple story problems from their math book. They read and reread each problem, struggling to understand what to do in order to solve the problem. Although I would help them with a particular problem, many students were never able to create a structure that would enable them to solve other problems. Of course, there were always a small number of students who seemed to possess a special kind of genius for solving story problems. Finally it occurred to me to ask them what they did. Almost without exception, these individuals used some form of mental imagery to understand the problem. So I began to ask students to visualize the components of each problem. I also showed them how to sketch simple illustrations that would help them see what they were being askeed to do. This visual approach to solving story problems has worked well. Students enjoy making the sketches and they now have a visual strategy that can be used whenever words get in the way.

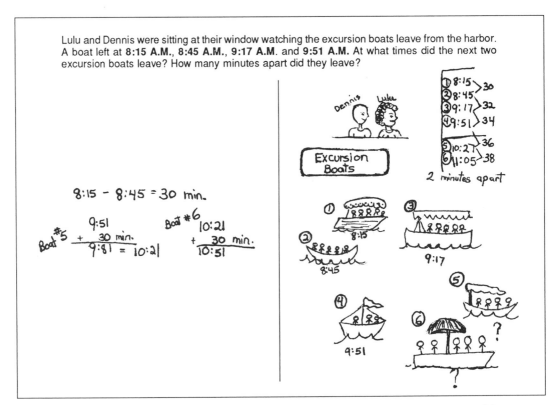

Lulu and Dennis were sitting at their window watching the excursion boats leave from the harbor. A boat left at **8:15 A.M.**, **8:45 A.M.**, **9:17 A.M.** and **9:51 A.M.** At what times did the next two excursion boats leave? How many minutes apart did they leave?

5th graders tackled this story problem. Work to the left of the line represents this student's first attempt to answer the problem. Work to the right of the line displays a visual approach to solving this problem. Two-thirds of the students in my classroom believe that illustrations helped them find the right answer to this problem.

It is essential that educators become knowledgeable about visual forms of thought. In the past we have mistakenly identified high intellectual accomplishment only with verbal and mathematical symbols. Now we must consider the implications of thought processes as described by Flemming, Watson, Tesla, and Einstein. Have we been shortchanging our students by our preoccupation with abstract, symbolic thought? Were we ourselves shortchanged as students? For me, the answer is a heartfelt DEFINITELY. The visual atrophy of my students, not to mention my own, has been exposed time and again. But I have found that it is possible to provide students with a whole education, one that balances symbolic thought with concrete image-thinking. In order to achieve this important balance, the following question must be explored:

What is visual thinking?

what is visual thinking?

Many words tie vision to thinking. Insight, foresight, hindsight, oversight, overview, preview, and visionary are examples. The very word idea derives from the Greek *idein* meaning to see. The following everyday phrases also link vision to thinking:

> Do you see what I mean?
> Let's examine the big picture.
> We will explore another viewpoint.

Visual thinking pervades all human activity. A driver maneuvers a car along an unfamiliar highway. A carpenter translates plans into things. Surgeons perform operations. People form first impressions of other people. Small children "read" pictures in storybooks. And, of course, visual thinking almost always precedes our selection of fruit and vegetables in a market.

In *Experience in Visual Thinking*, Robert McKim states that visual thinking is conducted by three kinds of visual imagery:

1. The images we see. (Note that people see images, not things.)
2. The images we imagine in our mind's eye.
3. The images we draw or paint.[4]

Visual thinking can take place primarily in the seeing mode, only in one's imagination, or with the use of paper and pencil. Individual thinking styles do vary. Some visual thinkers are most comfortable seeing three-dimensional images. Others prefer inner images. And still others think best when they are sketching their ideas. However, expert visual thinkers stretch their visual thinking style to include the use of all three kinds of imagery interchangeably. They recognize that when seeing, imagining, and drawing are utilized interactively, visual thinking can be experienced to a far greater extent.

The interactive nature of seeing, imagining, and drawing is portrayed on the preceding page. Overlapping circles indicate a wide variety of visual interactions. Where imagining and seeing overlap, seeing provides raw data for imagining while imagination expands and enriches seeing. Where drawing and imagining overlap, drawing nurtures and expresses imagining, while imagining provides the inspiration and ideas for drawing. Where seeing and drawing overlap, seeing assists drawing while drawing promotes active seeing.

An example of this interactive process can be seen in a 5th grade class studying action verbs. The teacher asks three students to pantomime a few examples of action verbs while the rest of the class watches and tries to guess which verb is being pantomimed. Students are then asked to define the term *action verb* by using lines and shapes rather than alphabet. Several students begin to make pencil marks on their paper, then pause to retreat into their imagination or to re-experience some of the verbs which were pantomimed. Within seconds they resume their sketch. Moving about among perceptual, inner, and

interactive visual thinking strategies

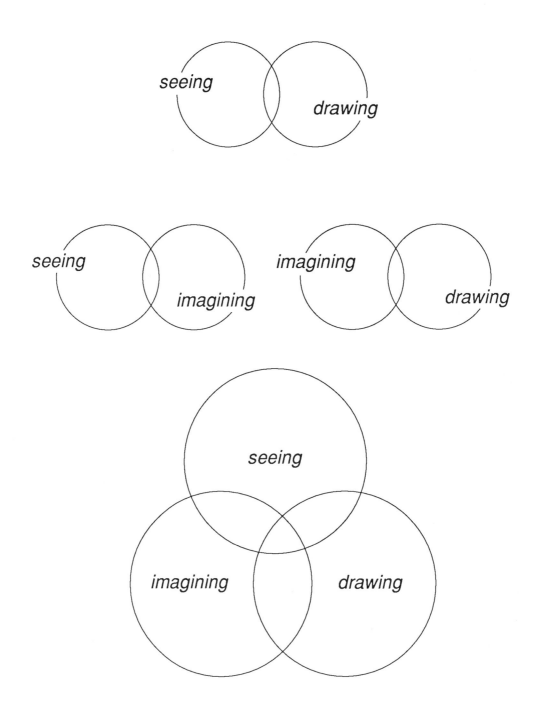

Based on the visual-thinking strategy model developed by Robert McKim.

see → draw

1. Students see and then draw the six different types of clouds. (Posters and/or film-strips can provide the seeing.)

2. Students look through a microscope at red blood cells, etc., and then draw what they see.

3. Students see a visual of the respiratory system and then draw their own.

see → imagine

1. Have the class study a map which outlines the voyage of Columbus or another explorer. Students then participate in a guided imagery about the voyage and discuss what they saw.

2. Students are shown a picture of the White House. Through guided imagery they take a tour through several rooms in the White House.

3. Each student is given a seed to observe. In an imagery exercise, students imagine themselves as the seed going through various growth stages.

imagine → draw

1. Students participate in an imagery about living in a big city (or the 20th century, etc.). Everyone then works in groups to create a mural based on what they experienced during the imagery.

2. Students (during imagery) become a water molecule and change from a solid to a liquid to a gas. Afterwards, everyone draws a water cycle diagram.

see → imagine → draw

1. Students observe visuals of many forms of transportation. Next they imagine their own unique form of transportation. This form of transportation is illustrated and displayed in the classroom.

2. The teacher cuts up one or more large flowers so that students can see and examine the parts. Then students participate in an imagery which allows them to see pollination from the inside of a flower. They watch as pollen grains enter the pollen tube to fertilize the egg cells and become new seeds. Finally, each learner draws a diagram of the parts of a flower.

graphic images, students continue until they are satisfied with their visual representations. The completed sketches vary, but their simple visual language shows the teacher that students are thinking about and therefore beginning to comprehend the definition of an action verb.

Drawing to extend one's thinking (graphic ideation) is often confused with drawing to communicate a well-formed idea (graphic commmunication). The former takes place before the latter. In fact the very process of idea sketching (graphic ideation) develops visual ideas worth communicating. In the classroom I often ask students to draw miniature murals which portray a concept such as alienation, unity, freedom, or conservation. Students have learned that a drawing of this nature is always preceded by an idea sketch. Scratch paper is made available for the idea sketch. Students quickly draw a series of partially formed ideas on their paper. Each little sketch evolves from the preceding sketch. The marks which appear on their paper are concerned more with the overall idea or concept than with details. These drawings are often cluttered and messy in appearance. When they have finished exploring the concept in this fashion, quality white drawing paper is provided for the final drawing. The completed drawings are displayed and shared. Some students portray a concept like interdependence in an abstract manner while others prefer to share their understanding of this idea with realistic drawings of people working together. The important fact remains that, abstract or realistic, the thought process has been visual.

There is no single way to learn to think visually. Certainly a step-by-step procedure is not recommended. For visual thinking does not always occur in a sequential manner whereby an individual sees an image, adds a touch of inner imagery, and then proceeds to draw a series of sketches. Visual thinking may begin with any of these three components and then spontaneously cycle through one or both of the others. Therefore, students need to learn to think visually in a flexible, open-ended manner. Any activity that causes students to examine their world more closely, use their imagination, and sketch their ideas provides valuable practice in visual thinking.

| Judicial | Legislative | Executive |

5th grade students were asked to illustrate the three branches of government. Initially the students sketched out their rough ideas (graphic ideation). Here is the final drawing (graphic communication) that was displayed in the classroom. Illustration by Mary Dicken.

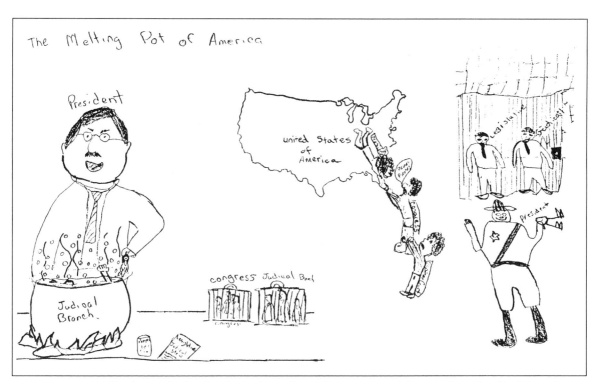

Students depict the three branches of government in a series of editorial cartoons. These cartoons show what could happen if one branch of government became too powerful. While these drawings help students to remember what the three branches of government are, the cartoons portray a deeper level of conceptual understanding about the three branches of government.

I have found that a strong visual arts program builds wonderful skills in visual thinking. Increased visual awareness, imagination, and freehand drawing are vital to artistic expression as well as visual thought. The units and activities described throughout the book are usually referred to as visual art experiences but I would also like you to think of them as experiences which build skill in visual thinking.

what is visual art?

A Traditional View of Visual Art: Perhaps no one, to this date, has been able to develop an adequate definition of art, one that will clearly and thoroughly answer the questions we can ask about it. However, some initial statements will help us begin to understand the nature of art. Art is "humanmade." What people make to be seen, if it is called art, must have importance or value to us. It must have meanings which cause the viewer to have thoughts and feelings and which make it stand out. The object must be of value for its own sake— not valuable only because it is of use to us. For example, an antique phonograph which no longer plays is important and valuable to look at even though it cannot be used. In *The Arts We See,* Vincent Lanier synthesizes the above statements in the following definition of art: "A work of visual art is a made object we see that we value for its own sake."[5]

In *Becoming Human Through Art*, Edmund Feldman offers another traditional definition of art by saying that ". . . it is a commodity with a market value."[6] Certainly it is fortunate that today the visual arts are so popular and available in the marketplace. But the status of art as property or as investment influences the way we perceive art objects and the work of artists. The successful promotion of art in our society has resulted in a strange irony: art seems less relevant to life even though it has become such a popular acquisition. By placing so much emphasis on art as a commodity, we have managed to move art to the outer periphery of our lives and imaginations.

An Expanded View of Visual Art: While art is still valued as an adornment of gracious living, times are changing. Many art educators remember and value the type of primitive art practiced by early tribespeople, an art created not to be exhibited in museums, in fact, rarely even made to be looked at. Rather, such art exists to be handled, worn, and carried. Because primitive peoples do not study art as we do, they make it and use it and often discard it. As the Balinese say, "We have no art. We do everything as well as we can."

The attitude of children toward their creations differs very little from the attitude of the tribesman toward his art. The function of art for the child may be fulfilled simply by the act of making. Or it may serve its purpose when it is shown to someone who then responds. After their creations have been "used," children often discard them. Thus, permanence is usually a matter of indifference for both the tribesman and the child. Another similarity between tribal art and that of young children stems from the fact that neither realize they are creating art. They draw and create three-dimensional forms quite spontaneously and without instruction.

We can learn so much from the viewpoint of primitive art, above all that our culture is afflicted by the separation of art and life. Perhaps art has been prevented from fulfilling its most important function by being honored too much. Fortunately schools and museums, especially in this country, have done much to overcome this isolation by making works of art more accessible and familiar. And yet, works of art are not the whole of art. In order to regain the timeless

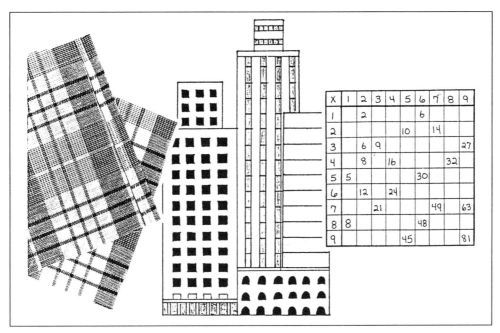

Seldom do teachers tell their students that the repeated fabric of their clothing is found in the windows of high rise office buildings and in the multiplication tables they labor to memorize.

X	1	2	3	4	5	6	7	8	9
1		2				6			
2					10		14		
3		6	9						27
4		8		16				32	
5	5					30			
6		12		24					
7			21				49		63
8	8					48			
9					45				81

benefits of art, we need to envision valued works of art as a symbol of a more universal effort to give visible form to all aspects of life. The accepted, traditional understanding of art must be expanded to include a psychological and educational approach that recognizes art as a visual form and visual form as the basis of productive thinking.

In *Visual Thinking*, Rudolf Arnheim states that there is a tendency to ". . . treat the arts as an independent area of study and to assume that intuition and intellect, feeling and reasoning, art and science coexist but do not cooperate."[7] Educators can and must act to end this separation within the curriculum. For in the act of creating and perceiving art, we rediscover a timeless mode of learning. "It is a mode of learning that naturally and organically unites knowing and doing; creating effects and judging their meaning; taking chances and calculating the consequences; erecting hypotheses and looking for confirmation; interfering with ideas and suggesting alternatives."[8]

By accepting the idea that art is not only a subject in the school curriculum but also a way of thinking and learning about life, we can do much to encourage the use of the visual arts as a mode of knowing. All knowledge is related, so we need to reach into the rich imagery of mathematics, science, and social studies to provide opportunities for art expression. Few teachers enable students to experience a circle as a mathematical, symbolic, functional, and beautiful form. Seldom do they tell their students that the patterns in the fabric of their clothing can be found in the windows of high-rise office buildings and in the multiplication tables they labor to memorize. Once it is understood that productive thinking in any area of cognition is perceptual thinking, the central function of art in education as well as in life will become obvious.

my own visual odyssey

"You teach best what you most need to learn" *Illusions,* Richard Bach

Richard Bach's quote has echoed through my mind many times. I began my first year of teaching in 6th grade with a lot of enthusiasm and a large cupboard filled with art supplies. After my own decidedly negative experiences in art, it surprised me when I began providing weekly art activities for my class. Ideas for these activities were gleaned from teacher magazines, art handbooks, and other teachers. While I did not actually teach art, I did provide simple clear directions with an example that I had made. Never did I give students a sheet of large white paper and ask them to simply draw something. How did my students respond? It was one of the high points of their week. Every Monday morning they would ask, "What are we doing in art this week?" As the year progressed it became more difficult to find "something different" for the next week's activity. However, I never disappointed them. It had become apparent to me that the painting, drawing, and constructing they did provided a much needed balance in our rigorous academic curriculum.

As the year progressed, I continued to be amazed at the "hold" art activities seemed to have over students. There was less absenteeism on art day. Those who were reluctant to finish a math or writing assignment on other days, always seemed to have their academic work done on this one day of the week. They knew I might insist that they finish their work before beginning art. (Today I no longer withhold art activities from students who have not completed an assignment. Many years ago I came to the conclusion that art is simply too important for anyone to miss — ever.)

When I asked a particular student why she enjoyed art, she responded by saying, "It's one of the few times we get a chance to play at school." I have always found that children draw a clear line between work and play. For most of them, art is an enjoyable form of play. And yet, when I observe students absorbed in an art project, the level of mental activity they expend appears to be tremendous. I often wished that this deep level of concentration could be transformed to other subjects as well. From my own point of view, some very productive work and play has taken place.

During my second year in the classroom I began to integrate art into other subject areas. Since students enjoyed art so much, it seemed wasteful to limit art time to one period per week. They created dioramas, clay masks, totem poles, and group murals in history. Paper skeletons and models of molecules originated from science units. Students also drew diagrams of almost everything we studied in science. Their reports, stories, and poems accompanied their own illustrations.

One day my principal visited the classroom during a 2nd period math lesson. My students were learning about the concept of multiplication by making individual paper weavings to represent a multiplication grid. Immediately I became anxious. Would he understand the significance of what we were doing? Or would he wonder why the students were doing a messy art activity during prime teaching time? Later that day I dropped by his office to talk about the lesson. He did not seem to be the least bit concerned about the active art-oriented nature of the lesson. In fact, I was encouraged to continue integrating art into my lessons. What a relief it was for me to have this support. The Back to Basics Movement had strongly influenced my thinking about classroom curriculum during the seventies. Standardized test scores all across the nation were dropping. In response to this, school districts throughout the nation promised to improve test scores by placing more emphasis on mastering the basics. Teachers were encouraged to stress drill, memorization, and home-work while art and music were seldom mentioned. I continued to teach art and integrate it into the curriculum but I always seemed to be looking over my shoulder, wondering if I could really justify spending so much time on art.

Then in 1979 Betty Edward's book, *Drawing on the Right Side of the Brain*, was published. I read her book several times, realizing that at last I could explain why art should be a vital part of every child's education. The idea that we all have two distinct ways in which to process information enabled me to purposely design classroom activities for both the verbal left mode as well as for the visual/spatial right mode. I began to give talks at local teacher conferences on hemisphericity so that more teachers would understand the importance of honoring the right mode thought processes of their students.

In 1980 I volunteered to serve on an art curriculum committee in our school district. When the committee convened, I learned that California's state guidelines for art education expected elementary teachers to do more than provide a variety of art experiences throughout the year. Teachers were now being asked to teach specific objectives which included helping students develop skill in the elements and principles of art.

In the beginning, this emphasis on direct instruction made me uncomfortable. I was not well-versed in the elements and principles of art. Also I was concerned that such formal instruction might interfere with the free-flowing spontaneity of student expression. However, I decided to coach myself in these fundamentals and then teach students about them. Before long my entire class had become knowledgeable about the characteristics of line and shape. They learned about the properties of color by creating their own color wheels. They also explored the subtle differences among various textures and learned how to create the illusion of actual texture with a pen or pencil. In addition, they were given some very basic instruction in freehand drawing which enabled them to express themselves with more confidence and pride. Although their teacher did not know how to draw, she learned as they learned. At the end of that school year I was no longer hesitant about teaching the elements and principles of visual art. It was obvious to me that direct instruction did not impede the creative process. On the contrary, it helped students acquire skills they needed to be their most creative, expressive selves.

I have continued to teach art as a discipline. Year after year students enter my classroom and acquire basic skills in visual arts. These skills are then used to explore important concepts in all subject areas. Their detailed drawings and colorful constructions displayed about the classroom reflect a visual way of thinking that students have learned to honor.

For some students, the ability to think visually comes naturally. Others are not as comfortable abandoning the structure of language, even temporarily. This truth became especially evident to me when I worked with an academically superior group of 4th grade students. Every year their teachers applauded the wonderful work they did. When they entered my classroom, I had to agree with their previous teachers. They were an intellectually elite group of young students. Most of them took great pride in the quality and accuracy of their written work. They wanted A's, only A's, and indeed the grade book began to bulge with them.

However, the second week of school I was surprised by their stilted efforts to create a line design. I had already introduced them to the basic characteristics of line and we had studied the use of line in well-known works of art. When they were given an opportunity to create their own line design, their usual confidence and decisiveness disappeared. Although I had shown some examples and given very clear directions, these students continued to ask for more direction. Finally I realized that they were afraid of doing it the "wrong way." Most of them finally did finish their line design but their final efforts lacked the usual spontaneity and creativity so typical of students their age. The next day we discussed the nature of artistic expression. I stressed the idea that there is no "right way" to do an art activity. Rather there is an infinite number of possibilities. Each of of us must find or create our own answer as we work.

In the weeks that followed, students did learn how to express themselves in an individual, creative way. Through discussion, the use of guided imagery, and participation in a variety of art activities, they became fluent in imagining and then constructing their own solutions. How I enjoyed watching them sketch their ideas on scratch paper before fashioning a collage or shaping a piece of clay. Often they would ask permission to go outside and take a closer look at a car, a tree, or a building. Students soon began to realize that the ability to shape a creative idea or solution is closely linked to their perceptual awareness of the environment. Those students who visually absorbed the everyday details of their world simply had more raw material with which to be creative. On many occasions they used the encyclopedia to study the contour of a particular animal or the facial features of a well-known figure. Eventually we began a class file of photographs that could be used as an ongoing visual reference. On one wall of the classroom, "What Do You See?" is displayed in large block letters during the first month of school. As students enter the classroom they are reminded to be more visually attuned to their own world.

As these 4th grade students learned to think and solve artistic problems in a visual way, I began to observe other benefits throughout the curriculum. In class discussions about history, literature, or science students became more com-fortable formulating answers to questions that did not have a single right answer. For example, I would ask them to imagine that gold had never been discovered in California. Then I would ask, "How might the history of California have been different?" Early in the year, this style of divergent thinking had perplexed them. They did not know how to handle such an open-ended thought process. They also struggled with writing an original poem or an imaginative story. As their skill in visual thinking increased, I began to notice the intellectual quality of class discussions improve. Students began to enjoy the challenge of "What if?" kinds of questions. After checking their comprehension of basic information in a given subject area, we were free to make new connections and explore the possibilities. Furthermore, their ability to write warm, witty poems, rich in metaphor and sensory detail, began to amaze and entertain us all.

The year I spent with those 4th graders will always be a kind of milestone for me. It was a time when I began to clearly see the powerful connections among visual thinking, art experiences, and creative thought. I now see that art is not only a fundamental part of the curriculum, but in fact essential to every student's intellectual development. In learning to express themselves visually, they also learn to express themselves in divergent thought forms that enable them to explore and develop original thinking in academic subject areas. These days I often find myself referring to art as the 4th R in the curriculum.

Anytime Dreams — Day or Night

I love to dream about fluffy white clouds
floating across the sky
... about trees gracefully swaying
in the wind
... about dancing and singing in
the forest

I love to dream about friends who care
and share their joy with me
... about parents who help me
grow in oh so many ways
... about teachers and leaders
who guide me through my early years

As you can see —
my dreams are magnificent and colorful

Julie McNulty

Sand

Sand, sand
Look at every grain
See it flowing
Through your hand

Stephen Campbell

Flowers, Beautiful and Sweet

The flowers are beautiful and sweet
With stems so green and petals so soft

To me they smell like peppermints
and freshly picked strawberries
The deep reds remind me of the stripes
on the American flag
Rich purples recall a basket of freshly
picked grapes
Sunny yellows tell of honey as it flows
from a bee hive
Bright oranges remind me of pumpkins
waiting in the field to be picked

Yes ...
the flowers are beautiful and sweet
With stems so green and petals so soft

Duane Iwamura

Candle Flames

When I look into a candle flame
I see ...
Robins flying way up high
And red dots forming in the sky
I see a warm winter night
while sitting by the firelight
I see leaves burning in the warm, warm sun
Or a roast, a roast well done
I see a river of gold
Or a seashell very old
I see lights in Las Vegas
And colors everywhere
I see diamonds glittering in the sun
And this is weird, but sometimes I even see
Matilda the Hun

Then my daze is gone
And my day is done

Matt Garcia

---

a prescription for
teaching visual thinking

At the beginning of every school year I bring to class a life-sized rubber brain, purchased in the educational section of a local toy store years ago. "My other brain," as I refer to it, is separated into four sections so that students can explore the interior. Because students enjoy handling the brain whenever possible, I often find myself or another student washing it at the back sink.

After the rubber brain has been passed around for a day or two, I begin a unit entitled "The Great Brain." It is not necessary to interest students in studying about the human brain. They have one of their own and that is all the motivation they need. At first we explore the anatomy of the brain, labeling each part and learning about what it does for us. Then we begin to talk about hemisphericity. On the model brain students have already observed the corpus callosum which connects the two halves of the brain. So when we discuss the differences in the operation of the left and right hemispheres of the brain, students have a visual-tactile impression of this phenomenon. I tell the class that the left side of the brain is primarily responsible for step-by-step reasoning, logic, mathematical ability, and speaking. By contrast, the right side of the brain may be described as visual/spatial, creative, and intuitive. To describe the personality of each hemisphere, we might way that the LH is serious-minded and judgmental about what it considers good or bad. The LH has learned a number of "truths" and it is not happy unless it can match new information to the old established patterns it knows and trusts. The playful RH is open-minded to most any new experience. The right side delights in forming unique, new patterns from seemingly unrelated bits of visual information. It can be said that the RH is submissive to the LH because the RH is often prevented from "doing its own thing" by the judgmental and sensible LH. New patterns of the world suggested by the RH are seldom given any credence by the LH. And yet, seeing and making new patterns is the very essence of fresh, creative ideas.
It does not take students long to see that they are relying on the LH of their brain during most of the school day. It also occurs to them, almost simultaneously, that they need more opportunities to use and develop the creative genius of their less recognized RH.

During "The Great Brain Unit," I hang up two large sheets of butcher paper on the back wall. One sheet is labeled RM activities (visual/spatial thinking) and the other sheet is labeled LM (verbal, logical thinking). Up until this time students have been talking about the differences in the brain. However, I now want them to understand that we cannot always be certain that the right hemisphere is solely responsible for creative ideas or that the Left Hemisphere handles their math assignments all by itself. Rather, the two sides of our brain work as partners, sending information back and forth through the corpus callosum. Since we can never be certain about which side of the brain should be given credit for our accomplishments, we now begin to talk about a right- and a left-mode way of experiencing the world. Students seem to have no difficulty adjusting to the implications of these new terms. So I challenge them to think of activities inside the classroom which favor RM thought. Art activities, music, P.E., recess, and eating lunch are often the only items students can think of to write on the butcher paper labeled RM activities. However, the butcher paper labeled LM activities is quickly filled. English, History, Reading, Math, writing reports, writing answers to questions, lessons taught by the teacher, class discussions, and tests are among the daily classroom activities listed. When the RM list is more complete, we talk about how activities which appear to favor the RM can be incorporated by the teacher into all subject areas. Poetry, creative writing, role-playing, games, visualization, demonstrations, music, and art add a rich RM dimension to all of the academic subjects students have listed on the LM chart.

After the class has been given an overview of the brain and hemisphericity, I explain that the best way to develop the creative gifts of RM visual thinking is by learning to:
1. **See** the colors, lines, shapes, and textures of our everyday world.
2. **Imagine** pictures or images in the mind's eye.
3. **Draw** their ideas freehand.

I tell them that we will be working on these goals throughout the year. Some students are very curious about how these goals will be accomplished. They have heard that Mrs. Mason does a lot of art but they are only beginning to realize that art will be much more than a random assortment of entertaining activities. In fact, students will learn that art, like reading or math, is a discipline with skills to be practiced and mastered.

Early in the year I introduce a series of activities that foster perceptual awareness. (Please refer to the section entitled "Developing Perceptual Awareness" for more specifics.) It is important for students to develop an increased awareness of all five senses, not just their visual sense, because the ability to see is polysensory. Ordinarily we do not make full use of our ability to see. It has often been said we look but do not see. A tremendous amount of knowledge can be gathered through direct visual perception. By becoming more attuned to all five senses, we begin to see the diverse details embedded in an individual image along with the larger generalized patterns we usually see.

When I am convinced that students are more aware of the particulars of their outside world, I have them visualize particular objects or scenes with their eyes closed. Many students have difficulty creating an inner mental image. Their mind's eye seems to be almost blind. However, using the practical exercises outlined in the section entitled "Building Mental Images for Visual Thinking," students can and do learn to experience some form of mind's eye imagery, so basic to visual thinking.

During the course of the year, students participate in a series of units relating to the elements and principles of art. These units, which appear later in the book, can be introduced in any order but my own preference is to begin with the unit on line. It seems to reinforce much of the work I do with students in perceptual awareness. The next unit I teach is Freehand Drawing. I feel that it is important to introduce this unit as early as possible during the year. Most students are not comfortable with their ability to draw. After this unit has been presented, they relax and begin to enjoy expressing their ideas in a visual form. Also, because I ask them to illustrate concepts and ideas in all subject areas throughout the year, they need to develop this skill early in the year.

The unit on freehand drawing is followed by the unit on shape. Lessons and activities in Shape/Form further enhance students' ability to see and draw. The unit on color, probably my favorite unit because color defines our world as well as our individual lives in so many beautiful ways, is next. The last unit to be introduced is texture. Students enjoy working with a variety of textures. I do not believe any of us ever outgrow our need to feel the world with our hands and eyes.

While the units on line, freehand drawing, shape, color, and texture are in progress, I freely integrate the visual arts into all subject areas. For example, when the year begins, students learn to punctuate and categorize sentences in the English book. Although this technical information is essential, the sentences they write in their stories and daily work are usually dull and lacking in detail. So we leave the English book for two days and create a diamond mine. I hang a sheet of black butcher paper on the back wall to represent the dark interior of the mine. Then students begin to draw diamonds in every imaginable size and shape. Each paper diamond is mounted on the black paper, producing a spectacular final effect. On the following day I read aloud several unrelated sentences, one at a time. Some of the sentences are, like the diamonds, true gems, rich in imagery and colorful in detail. Others are just ordinary sentences. Students are then asked how a sentence is sometimes like a diamond. After they have made the connection, everyone writes original diamond sentences on strips of paper that can be mounted alongside their diamonds in the mine. The sentences they create for the mine definitely have a sparkle of their own. As they go on to write paragraphs and full length stories, I occasionally remind them to include some diamond sentences.

Throughout the year students continually experience a shift between visual and verbal thinking. Visual thinking complements verbal thinking by bringing us closer to concrete reality. The graphic image of a circle, for example, is clearly more concrete in meaning than the word *circle*. Because visual imagery is more concrete than words or numbers, students need to access it on a daily basis. In doing so they become ambidextrous in their thinking: using verbal, logical LM thought as well as visual/spatial RM thought. Thinkers who cannot escape the structure of language never realize their full potential as learners. As Arthur Koestler states in *The Act of Creation*, "Language can become a screen that stands between the thinker and reality."[9]

around the wheel with visual art

ou and your students will develop increased skill in visual thinking as you journey around these wheels together. To create these wheels, I decided to work with five of the art elements: line, shape, form, color, and texture. Below is a brief definition for each of the five elements:

Line: The path made by a moving point. Lines are often suggested, rather than drawn. They vary in characteristics and emotional effects.

Shape: The area enclosed when a line returns to touch itself. A flat two-dimensional area which is given importance by line, color or texture.

Form: A three-dimensional area which has height, width and depth. It may be viewed from all sides.

Color: White light contains all of the known colors, and we often consider light and color one element. Study of color includes shading, color formulation, and the psychological effects of color.

Texture: The tactile quality of an object. Texture may be actual or visual. As you will notice, I have combined shape and form as the subject of one wheel. I made a decision to do this because I wanted students to experience the relationship between these two elements. In addition to the five elements of art, I have also included a freehand drawing wheel because drawing is an essential visual thinking strategy.

I did not include any wheels concerning the principles of art. The following art principles are often referred to during my art lessons and in the future it would be a wonderful idea to create wheels for them as well. In any case, please refer to these principles often. They are also important aspects of visual thought.

Rhythm: Rhythm is a graceful flowing movement or a continuity achieved by repetition. When color and forms are repeated with irregular variations, the result is more dynamic than when the repeat is regular.

Balance: Balance is a state or condition of equilibrium. It is an arrangement in which equal forces neutralize each other.

Proportion: Proportion is the comparative relationship between a whole and its parts and among the parts themselves.

Contrast: Contrast is a sharp difference of size, shape, color value or texture among parts of a composition.

These visual art wheels can be adapted to meet the needs of almost any grade level or teaching situation. Perhaps you will wish to create your own visual art wheels. If so, refer to Bernice McCarthy's books cited in the bibliography.

As can be seen in the photograph of the house, lines are all around us and can be found anywhere.

line

Line is the most basic element in art. The scrawling lines made by small children are their first attempts at sharing with others what they see. Through continued experimentation, children explore artful ways to express themselves with line. However, as they leave the primary grades, students often become critical of their drawings. They want their picture of a horse or landscape scene to look like the real thing. For this to happen, young artists will need to become more aware of the lines in their environment. Only then will they be able to use them more realistically in their drawings.

One way to foster an increased sensitivity to line is by collecting "lines" that can be displayed in the classroom. Wire whisks, coat hangers, paper clips, and balls of string are some of the more obvious examples of line that first make their way into the collection. Later, items such as old shoes, a piece of cloth, a family photograph, or perhaps a potted plant are added. As the collection grows, students see that everything has lines and that lines can be light, dark, harsh, soft, clear, blurred, curved, or straight. Some lines are manmade while others are designed by nature.

The Swiss artist Paul Klee once said that a line is a point taking a walk. Although a line has width, it is usually so much longer than it is wide that we think mainly about its length and direction. For example, a human hair normally appears to us as a line. However, under a microscope it is transformed into a shape. Thus, we might find ourselves wondering—is it a line or is it really a narrow shape? This is a question which I ask students about one or more of the objects in the line collection. As they share their ideas, it is clear that they are becoming more aware of line.

Lines can be thought of as a visual language. They can communicate the inner thoughts and feelings of the person who created them. For example, everyone's handwriting is unique because of the different ways of holding the pencil, different pressures applied to it, and differences in the way the letters are shaped. This explains why people who have previously seen your writing can often tell it is yours without reading what is written. From your handwriting people can also form a personal impression of you that is independent of the words and sentences you use. These same differences in line are found in drawings and paintings. However, the artist may purposely use line to create these differences.

In *Drawing On The Artist Within*, Betty Edwards introduces her readers to the language of line by having them do analog drawings. To make an analog drawing, students draw lines, only lines, which visually portray the meaning of a word or concept. In the unit on line which follows, I have included an activity which is adapted from Betty's book. Students of all ages will enjoy creating their own visual interpretation of concepts like joy, anger, peacefulness, or confusion. Lines flow easily onto paper as students discover a rich inner vocabulary.

Too often we hurry through our day, unaware of the soft lines on a rose, the grain of wood revealed in an oak table, or the expressive lines in the faces of people we see everyday. We must learn to experience the now. It may take some practice to quiet the chatter of our minds. But when we do allow ourselves to be more "connected" to the lines around us, we enrich our lives and the creative work we do.

Line *Line* *Line* *Line* *Line*

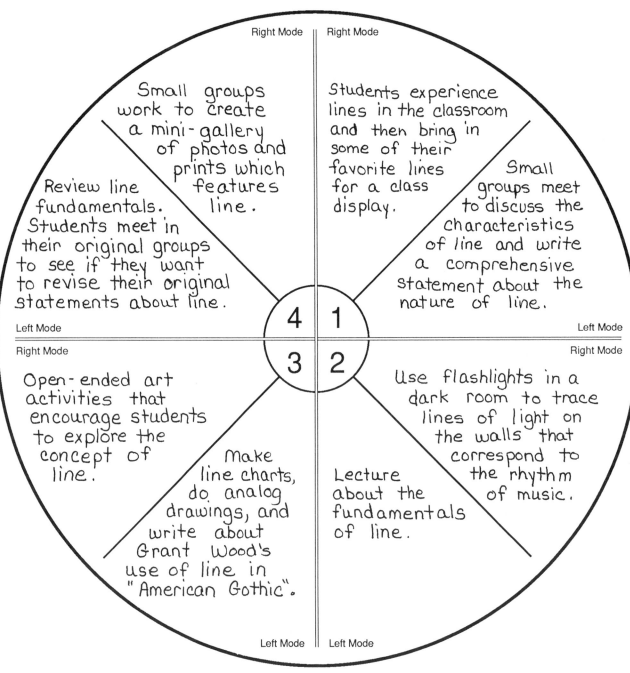

Right Mode | Right Mode

1 — Students experience lines in the classroom and then bring in some of their favorite lines for a class display.

1 (Left Mode) — Small groups meet to discuss the characteristics of line and write a comprehensive statement about the nature of line.

2 (Right Mode) — Use flashlights in a dark room to trace lines of light on the walls that correspond to the rhythm of music.

2 (Left Mode) — Lecture about the fundamentals of line.

3 (Left Mode) — Make line charts, do analog drawings, and write about Grant Wood's use of line in "American Gothic".

3 (Right Mode) — Open-ended art activities that encourage students to explore the concept of line.

4 (Left Mode) — Review line fundamentals. Students meet in their original groups to see if they want to revise their original statements about line.

4 (Right Mode) — Small groups work to create a mini-gallery of photos and prints which features line.

Based on the 4Mat system model by Bernice McCarthy.

BEYOND WORDS

Lines Quadrant I — Why?

1. Right Mode — Create an Experience

Objective:

To create a line collection and display it in the class.

Activity:

Always begin with what is most immediate for the child, lines in the world they know. For several days before the actual lesson, have them notice lines in the classroom, at home, on the playground. Then ask students to bring a variety of lines to be displayed on a table and/or bulletin board. Continue collecting every conceivable type of line for one week. Shoe strings, wire, straws, and combs are often a part of line collections but you may be surprised by some of the other items students bring. Fortunately students often become competitive as they strive to bring in the most unusual or surprising example of line.

Evaluation:

The number and variety of lines collected and the percentage of students who participate.

2. Left Mode — Analyze the Experience

Objective:

To discuss and write a comprehensive statement about the nature of line.

Activity:

Students gather in groups of four or five and discuss the characteristics of line. Each group makes a list entitled "What We Know About Line." When the list is completed, every group writes one comprehensive statement about the nature of line that can be shared with the class. After the statements have been shared, they should be saved for future reference.

Evaluation:

The quality of the comprehensive statement about line.

Lines Quadrant II — What?

3. Right Mode — Integrate Reflections into Concepts

Objective:

To further interiorize the meaning of line and to feel/see its movement.

Activity:

Students may be accustomed to thinking of line as a stationary mark or object. However, lines can and do move in many directions. Ask the class to close their eyes and imagine the movement made by the spokes on the bicycle tire or needle on a sewing machine. Now have students use small pocket flashlights in a dark room to trace lines of light. Play music while they make light lines that correspond to the rhythm. Let them pretend they are race horses going around a track, faster and faster, until the race is won. Change the music and they are old, worn jalopies sputtering down the road until they die. This is kinetic art. It lasts only a moment and is never the same again.

Evaluation:

The enjoyment of the students and any insights the experience has produced.

4. *Left Mode — Develop Theories and Concepts*

Objective:

To learn the definition of line. To learn about the kinds, characteristics, and uses of line.

Activity:

Present a lecture on line that introduces some or all of the material listed below. Before the lecture begins, you will want to hang a series of art prints that feature line. The following artists are noted for the use of line in their work: Albrecht Durer, M. C. Escher, Paul Klee, Pablo Picasso, Wassily Kandinsky, Willem de Kooning, and Alberto Giacometti.

About Line . . .

1. Line is one of the art elements.
2. A line is the path of a moving dot.
3. There are natural and manmade lines.
4. Lines can be characterized by their structure, direction, and movement.
   a. The structure of a line can be straight, angular, or curving.
   b. Line can move in a vertical, horizontal, diagonal, or circular direction.
   c. A line by its own definition moves somewhere.
5. Lines have many uses.
   a. They can be used to decorate surfaces.
   b. Lines define the edges of a shape or the contours of a form.
   c. Curving, angular, or straight lines can generate the illusion of movement or stillness.
   d. Lines are used to show texture.

6. The following design principals can be achieved with line: Contrast, Repetition, Balance, Perspective, Directional Eye Movement and Proportion.
7. Lines can be used to express an emotion as well as to visualize an idea, concept, or memory.

Evaluation:

Objective quiz.

Lines Quadrant III — How?

5. Left Mode — Working on Defined Concepts

Objective:

To review the characteristics of line by making a line chart. To use line as a form of expression by making four analog drawings. To write about Grant Wood's expressive use of line in "American Gothic."

Activity:

The three activities outlined below will require two or three periods to complete. During the first period, students make a line chart. This is a teacher directed activity and each step should be modeled on the board or overhead. The second activity, Analog Drawing, is based on an exercise described in *Drawing on the Artist Within* by Betty Edwards. As students use line to reflect their feelings about anger and joy, they learn how easily line can make inner thought visible. When students have successfully completed the line chart and the analog exercise, they have acquired the visual skill necessary to study and respond to Grant Wood's use of line in "American Gothic."

Making a Line Chart

1.	2.	3.	4.
5.	6.	7.	8.

figure 1

What You Need:
White paper (9 x 12 or 12 x 18)
Crayons

What To Do:
Provide each student with a sheet of paper and crayons. Students fold their paper to make 8 parts as shown in Figure 1. The boxes are numbered from one to eight. Give the following directions as students work to complete the chart.

1. Lines show varied, distinguishing characteristics. They can be horizontal or vertical. In box #1 make some horizontal and vertical lines and write the name for each type of line. Which lines give the impression of alertness? Which lines appear serene and calm?

2. Lines can be slanted or diagonal. Write the word diagonal at the top of box #2 and make some diagonal lines in this space.

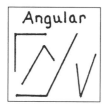

3. The angle line is made from two straight lines joining at some point. An angle can be very thin and narrow or very wide and open. Make some angles in box #3.

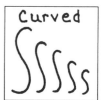

4. The lines you have made in boxes #1, #2 and #3 are straight lines. Lines can also be curved. Write the word curved at the top of box #4 and make some curved lines. Find some curved lines in the classroom.

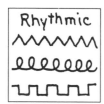

5. Lines can be rhythmic. Rhythmic lines repeat a pattern and often generate a feeling of movement. Label box #5 rhythmic and make some rhythmic lines.

6. Lines can be thick or thin. Write thick or thin at the top of box #6 and draw some of these lines.

7. Lines can be light or dark. Label box #7 light or dark. Make some light and dark lines.

8. The objects you see are often represented by combinations of straight, angular, or curving lines. Draw a simple figure in box #8 that uses all three kinds of lines.

1. anger	2. joy
3. peacefulness	4. confusion

figure 2

Drawing Analogs

What You Need:
White drawing paper (9x12 or 12x18)
Pencils
A collection of analog drawings that you can share with your students.

What To Do:
Provide each student with paper and pencil. Then read the following instructions aloud, giving students time to complete one step before going on to the next.

student analog drawings

Anger   Joy   Peacefulness   Confusion

1. Divide your sheet of paper into four sections. Number each section as shown in Figure 2. Label section #1 anger, section #2 joy, section #3 peacefulness, and section #4 confusion.

2. Use a pencil for these drawings. Each drawing will be made of lines. You may want to use one line or many lines.

3. Complete one section at a time. Make a drawing that represents what the word in that section stands for. Your drawing will express your inner thoughts about anger, joy, peacefulness, and confusion by giving them a visible form. There is one restriction. *Do not* draw any pictures or use any symbols. Rainbows, hearts, birds, and flowers are out. Use only the expressive language of line.

4. Read the word anger in section #1. Remember the last time you were really angry. Feel within yourself what that anger was like. Allow that anger to flow from you and find its way into the marks that are being made on your paper. The marks look like the anger you are feeling. They can be changed or erased if necessary to portray an image of anger as it feels to you.

5. Take as long as you need to complete these drawings. There is no right or wrong when you create analog drawings. Each image you make will be right because it is right for you. Do not try to visualize beforehand what the completed drawing will be like. Let the image emerge in its own way as the marks appear on your paper. Please finish all four analog drawings and then we will talk about how to read the language of line.

When students have completed the four analog drawings, tell them it is time to talk about the vocabulary of visual language. Using the overhead projector, show them some analog drawings that represent anger. (You may wish to make overheads of the examples in the book or you may wish to work with a few teachers and/or students to make some samples.) Students will notice that the lines which portray anger are heavy, dark, and jagged. However, the lines which portray joy tend to be light, curved, and rising. Discuss the similarities that can be found in your students' drawings of peacefulness. Then look for similar lines in the drawings that represent confusion. When you are confident that students can see the "family" resemblances shared by the drawings in each category, ask them to begin looking at the differences. No two analog drawings of anger will be exactly the same. Each individual experiences anger in a way that is different in quality, intensity, duration, and so on. Display several analog drawings of anger and encourage students to comment on these differences.

Lines portray inner thoughts and feelings in a way that makes it possible to intuitively know what is being expressed by another person. It might be possible to put this visual knowing into words. However, drawings contain so much complexity that it would be a tremendous task to put it all into words. As an experiment, ask your students to find appropriate words to express the meaning of one of their analog drawings. This will be a most difficult task. However, the experience is worthwhile because students become more sensitive to the differences between visual and verbal knowing. Students need to become well acquainted with the vocabulary of line so that they can "read" the meaning that is conveyed by the universal language of drawings.

For more information about analog drawing, please refer to Chapter 7 "Drawing Out Insight" in Betty Edward's book , *Drawing on the Artist Within.*[10]

Reading the Lines in Grant Wood's "American Gothic"

Display a large print of "American Gothic." Share some background information about Wood before asking students to examine Wood's use of line in writing.

Background Information:

> Grant Wood was born in 1891 on a farm north of Cedar Rapids, Iowa. When he was born, the first thing his father said was, "It's lucky he's Chunky. He'll make a good farmer." Young Grant grew up in the country surrounded on all sides by fields and sky. There were no telephones, cars, radios, or even electricity in his world.

> Wood painted his life. "American Gothic," done in 1930, appealed to nearly everyone. America plunged into the Great Depression, leaving many people jobless and homeless. Hard times made Americans value their roots and the traditional values of home and family. Grant Wood and other midwestern painters reaffirmed these values and became known as "American Regionalists."

> While Grant Wood was looking at a small farmhouse one day, he envisioned the house with a tightlipped pioneer couple standing in front of it. He used an old envelope to make a sketch of it. Then he asked his 30 year-old married sister Nan and his 62 year-old dentist to pose for him. When the painting was completed, it was sent to an exhibition at the Art Institute of Chicago. Grant won his first grand prize and the museum bought the painting for $600. Grant stated that "American Gothic" is a portrait of the people with whom he had grown up, who clung to the values of the past. "I wanted to paint that bleak, faraway, timeless quality in the eyes of my father and mother—the severe but generous vision of the midwest pioneer."[11] "American Gothic" has now gone beyond its own time and place to become an enduring symbol of America.

The Written Assignment:

> Tell students to study "American Gothic" carefully before they begin writing. Have them list the different kinds of lines they see (straight, angular, or curving) and the direction of the lines (horizontal, vertical, or diagonal). Ask the class to consider which type of line appears most often. Now give students an opportunity to write a paragraph or two about what the lines in "American Gothic" express. The line chart, the analog drawings, and the background information about "American Gothic" will help students to write about the visual language in this painting.

Evaluation:

How well students followed directions to complete a line chart and four analog drawings. The quality of student writing about the use of line in "American Gothic."

6. Right Mode — "Messing Around"

Objective:

To participate in two art activities that give students an opportunity to use their knowledge of line creatively.

Activity:

The following art activities enable students to explore line by having some fun with it. The Soft Line Design provides an opportunity for students to experiment with one or more of the design principles. The Two-Handed Drawing is an activity that focuses on the use of line for decoration.

Soft Line Design

What You Need:
Pencil
Yarn in many colors
Bottles of white glue
Paper (9x12 or 12x18)
Scissors

What To Do:
1. Review the principles of design and ask students to use one or more of them as they make a soft line design. Pass out a sheet of paper, a pair of scissors, and a bottle of glue to each student. Designate 3 or 4 tables about the classroom as yarn centers. Place several skeins of yarn in each center.

2. Tell students to lightly sketch a variety of interesting lines on their sheet of paper. Explain that the lines should be arranged to form a pleasing design and not a recognizable object. When students begin sketching, dismiss small groups to go to the yarn centers and gather the yarn they will need.

3. When students have finished sketching their lines, ask them to go over each line with glue and then lay a piece of yarn over the glue lines.

4. Students should continue gluing pieces of yarn until they are satisfied with their design.

5. Display the completed designs. Discuss any student use of the design principles. Ask students if any of the line designs seem to express a feeling or idea.

Two Handed Drawing

What You Need:
White drawing paper (12x18)
Crayons
Masking Tape
Scissors

What To Do:
Tell students that line can be just for decoration. Show pictures or actual examples of Persian rugs, Turkish mosques, and Chinese pagodas. Encourage students to notice the moldings, gingerbread, fluted column, and fancy ironwork that are a part of local buildings. Now pass out paper, two strips of making tape per student, and crayons or markers. Give students the following directions. Be sure to model step #2 on the chalkboard or on a large sheet of butcher paper.

figure 3

1. Tape the drawing paper to your desk.

2. Take a crayon or marker in each hand. Start at the top of the paper and make a mirror picture down the long side of your paper. See Figure 4. (Students will be surprised by the ability of one hand to follow in mirror fashion the direction of the other hand. Ask them which hand is the leader and which hand is the follower.)

3. Use the crayons to decorate the inside of your drawing with a splendid array of lines. (See Figure 3.)

At the close of this activity, make an impressive display by taping all two-

figure 4

handed drawings together across the ceiling or walls of the classroom. Have students study the drawings to notice how lines are used as decoration. Ask them to choose one they especially like and explain their reason for selecting it.

Evaluation:

Did students use a rich variety of lines to complete a soft line design and a two-handed drawing?

Lines Quadrant IV — If?

7. *Left Mode — Analyzing their own application of the concepts for useful ness, originality, and as a stepping stone for future learning.*

   Objective:

   To review what has been learned about the concept of line and reexamine the original group statements written about line.

   Activity:

   Display the comprehensive group statements that were written about line in Quadrant I. Have students comment on these statements. A great deal of material about line has been presented and experienced in Quadrants II and III. It is likely that some or all of the group statements have become dated. Allow time for students to meet with their group and rethink their original statement about the nature of line. Provide large sheets of paper for the groups who wish to rewrite their line statement. Display the newly written statements and have each group explain their revisions to the class.

   Evaluation:

   The quality of the final comprehensive statements and the class discussion about them.

8. *Right Mode — Doing it themselves and sharing what they do with others*

   Objective:

   To create and share a mini-gallery of photos and prints that feature line.

   Activity:

   Students have practiced "reading" the lines in Grant Wood's "American Gothic" and in other well-known works of art introduced in the lecture. Now it is time for them to begin observing and reading the lines in their daily lives. Have students work in groups to create a mini-gallery of current every day photos and prints gathered from magazines, newspapers, postcards, greeting cards, and personal photo collections. Each group should choose a topic or theme and collect only pictures which illustrate their chosen subject area. The following examples are often used for a theme study:

famous people	transportation
ordinary people	sports
children	dreams
families	landscapes
Animals	
-horses	
-cats	
-dogs	

Students should collect a minimum of five photos or prints and mount them on a large sheet of poster board or chart paper. Group members then study the use of lines in each picture to determine the message and/or mood. Each entry in the gallery is given a title and a caption based on what the lines "say." Every group will share their mini-gallery with the class and leave it on display in the classroom.

Evaluation:

The quality of prints and photos collected and the display itself.
The appropriate selection of titles and captions for each picture.

Freehand Drawing

The skill of freehand drawing can be acquired through direct instruction. Today many people still assume that drawing is a magical ability which only a few fortunate individuals seem to possess. While this attitude contributes to an appreciation of artists and their work, it does little to encourage the average person to learn to draw. In fact, people often believe that they should not take a drawing class unless they already know how to draw. In *Drawing on the Right Side of the Brain* by Betty Edwards, she demystifies the process of learning to draw.[12] Betty shows how simple exercises make it possible to teach drawing to anyone who is willing to try. Furthermore, the classroom teacher can help students learn this skill even though he/she may have little if any drawing skill.

The following unit will serve as a guide for teaching all of your students to draw. Take the necessary time to introduce students to all of the activities on the wheel. With some modification, students in the primary grades as well as adults can benefit from the instruction. Let students know that drawing is learning how to "see." Play the visual perception games introduced in Quadrant III and know that the time you spend on visual exercises is at least as important as the time spent drawing. The old expression, "I can't even draw a straight line" encourages people to believe that the ability to draw is related to coordination. Once your students learn to "see" the way artists do, they will discover that any person with average eyesight and eye-hand coordination can learn to draw.

As the unit begins, be sure to provide each student with a folder. Ask students to keep all of their drawings, dating each of them. They will enjoy a tremendous sense of accomplishment as they watch their individual style and skill in drawing develop. When you have completed all eight steps of the wheel, be sure your students continue to draw. Weave drawing experiences throughout all areas of the curriculum. Ask them to draw what they see under a microscope, the key elements in a story problem. a sequence of events in a story from the reading text, or an important happening in history.

In addition, plan a routine of five minute "drawing breaks" in the classroom. They will help children to continue developing their visual powers and their confidence in visually expressing objects, ideas, and events. Drawing breaks also provide a solution for those moments in the day when everyone needs a break, when too much cognitive processing has left teachers and students on edge. You will find that these breaks become "centering" experiences. Students become very quiet as they concentrate on the object drawn. Afterwards, they return to the regular routine relaxed and ready for the rest of their academic day

As you continue to provide drawing experiences throughout the year, realize that you are building a foundation that will serve your students well throughout life. By learning to draw, we develop the building blocks of visual perception, visual/spatial organization, and visual discrimination. Our brains cannot help but transfer these skills to reading or spelling, which require visual attention to detail as well as pattern and organization in space.

Once your students learn to "see" the way artists do, they will discover that any person with average eyesight and eye-hand coordination can learn to draw.

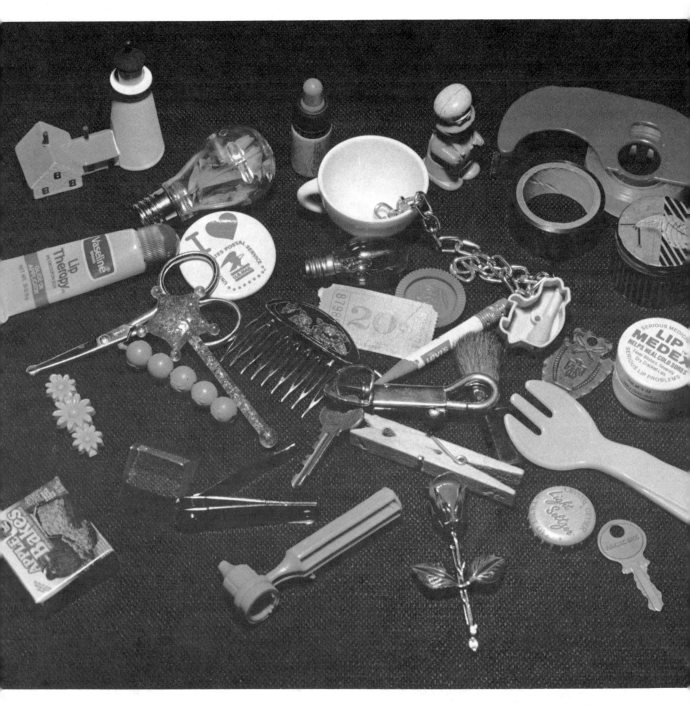

Place a collection of small objects in a box. Have students select one to draw whenever time permits.

BEYOND WORDS

Freehand Drawing

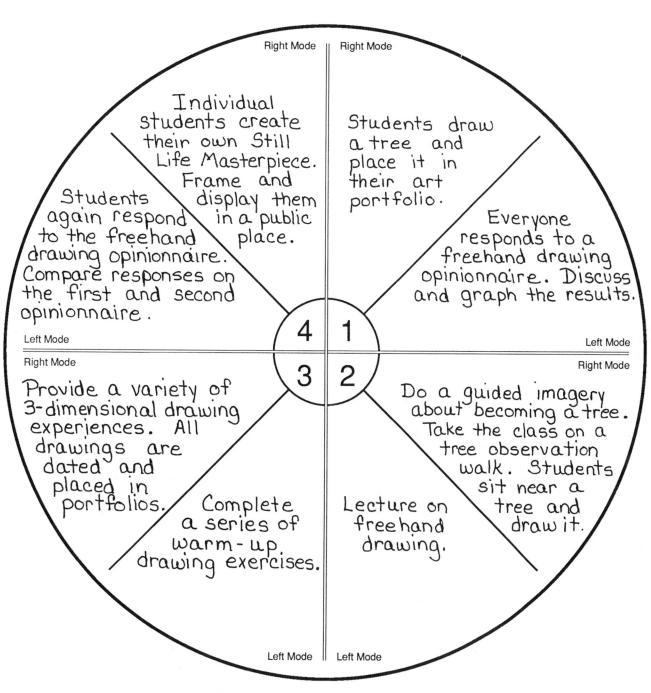

Right Mode | Right Mode

1 Students draw a tree and place it in their art portfolio.

Everyone responds to a freehand drawing opinionnaire. Discuss and graph the results.

Left Mode

Individual students create their own Still Life Masterpiece. Frame and display them in a public place.

Students again respond to the freehand drawing opinionnaire. Compare responses on the first and second opinionnaire.

Left Mode

4 1
3 2

Right Mode

Provide a variety of 3-dimensional drawing experiences. All drawings are dated and placed in portfolios.

Complete a series of warm-up drawing exercises.

Left Mode

Do a guided imagery about becoming a tree. Take the class on a tree observation walk. Students sit near a tree and draw it.

Lecture on freehand drawing.

Left Mode

Based on the 4MAT system model by Bernice McCarthy.

Freehand Drawing Quadrant I — Why?

1. Right Mode — Create an Experience

Objective:

Students will draw a tree from their imagination.

Activity:

Prepare an art portfolio for each student. The portfolios may be as simple as a set of individual file folders where students can go to file their drawings. When this has been accomplished, students are ready to begin their first drawing. Pass out sheets of 9x11 white drawing paper and tell students to draw a tree. They may draw any type of tree they have seen or can imagine. Do not provide any pictures, photos, or sketches to assist them. Also refrain from discussing characteristics of trees. Drawing a tree from memory and/or imagination will be a difficult and uncomfortable task for many. Older students are often self-conscious and do not want anyone to see what they have drawn. When students have completed their drawings, ask them to place their dated drawing in the portfolio.

Evaulation:

The completion of a tree drawing by each student.

2. Left Mode — Analyze the Experience

Objective:

Students will respond to a Freehand Drawing Opinionnaire and discuss the results.

Activity:

While the experience of drawing a tree from memory is still fresh in their minds, distribute individual copies of the Freehand Drawing Opinionnaire shown below.

Explain that an opinionnaire is a type of survey which can be used to measure public opinion about a particular topic. There are no right or wrong answers, just opinions. Tell students to place a true or false beside each statement. When the opinionnaire has been completed by everyone, tally the number of true and false responses for each statement. Record these responses on a vertical bar graph which shows the comparison of true and false responses for each statement. Then discuss each statement on the opinionnaire with the class. Analyze the meaning of a true response as well as the meaning of a false response for each item. During the discussion, refer to the tree drawing exercise and encourage students to share their thoughts about this experience. Connect this experience to some of the opinionnaire statements. Finally draw some conclusions about the overall opinion of the class concerning freehand drawing. Have students place the opinionnaire in their portfolio for future reference. Also save a copy of the bar graph.

Freehand Drawing Opinionnaire

Directions: Read each statement below. Write the word true on the line in front of each statement you agree with. Write the word false on the line in front of each statement with which you do not agree.

1. _____ The ability to draw well is a talent some of us are born with.

2. _____ Drawing lessons should only be given to those who show talent.

3. _____ An artist must be able to draw a straight line.

4. _____ There is a right and wrong way to draw.

5. _____ Real artists do not rely on pictures or photographs for ideas. They draw entirely from their imagination.

Evaluation:

Quality of the class discussion about the opinionnaire.

Freehand Drawing Quadrant II —What?

3. *Right Mode — Integrate Reflections into Concepts*

Objective:

To participate in a guided imagery and a tree walk that will enable students to experience "treeness."

Activity:

The following activity is designed to help students see trees the way an artist does. It is likely that many of the tree drawings completed earlier by your students are awkward and lacking in detail. Trees are difficult to draw well and older students often become frustrated as they attempt to draw "a real tree." Do the following guided imagery entitled "Becoming a Tree" with your students. Then take the class on a tree observation walk at your school or in a nearby park. Ask students to look closely and carefully at the trees and verbalize what they see. Afterward, have children sit near a tree and draw it. The guided imagery and the tree walk will provide students with the needed background and inspiration to improve their second tree drawing. When students have finished drawing a tree, provide space for them to display their first and second drawing. Some students may not feel comfortable displaying their drawings so this part of the activity needs to be strictly optional.

"Becoming a Tree"

Imagine you are a seed moving through the air. Allow the wind to carry you wherever it will...floating...twirling about...The wind is calmer now. See yourself drifting to the ground. Soon you will find yourself lying underneath the ground in cool, dark soil.... You seem to be all alone. Then you feel something damp surrounding your outer self. It is a spring rain that has dampened the earth and trickled down into the soil. You absorb some of this water, growing in size until your skin breaks open. A small root sinks deep into the soil while an upward stem breaks through the roof of the packed soil, reaching up to catch a ray of sunshine. Though very small, you are a tree. Feel the warm air and the gentle breeze. Years pass by as you grow into a strong young tree. Taller and taller you grow...Your branches extend and thicken until you have become a full-grown tree. What kind of tree are you? Admire yourself...the texture of your bark and the way in which each branch reaches out into the world. Notice the way your leaves or needles stir gently during a gentle breeze. You are truly a magnificent tree.

Evaluation: The completion of a second set of tree drawings which reflect student growth in learning to look closely and carefully at a tree.

4. Left Mode — Develop Theories and Concepts

Objective:

To explore the notion that learning to see is learning to draw.

To learn how the specialized functions of the right mode can help you and your students learn to draw.

To become familiar with simple exercises and activities that will improve student drawing ability.

Activities:

Present a lecture on freehand drawing which addresses some or all of the information contained in items one through six. Students in the primary grades will benefit most from instruction on The Basic Elements of Shape. (See item three.) Older students should become well acquainted with the structural and functional differences in the left and right side of their brain. Before the lecture begins, make individual copies of The *Basic Elements of Shape* chart for each student and make an enlarged copy of it for display in the classroom. Also find or make a large diagram of the brain which shows how the corpus callosum connects the left and right hemispheres. Now you are ready to begin.

1. *Drawing is a natural, human response.* Evidence of this can be found in caves and in tombs where Egyptians buried their god Kings. In almost every culture we know, people draw. They draw what they see as important in their daily lives. However, in our culture, drawing has no such value. It is considered play, something children do until they go to school to learn to read and write. Primary students are given some opportunities to draw but by high school it is almost completely eliminated from the curriculum. Nevertheless, drawing is a natural response and our brain is still programmed to draw.

   -What if all students were given an opportunity to study freehand drawing throughout school?

   -What if drawing had value as a way to communicate?

   -What would happen to the brains of human beings if they were stimulated and educated through regular periods of freehand drawing?

2. *Any person with average eyesight and eye-hand coordination can learn to draw.* Manual skill is not a key factor in learning to draw. Anyone who can write legibly has the necessary dexterity to draw well.

3. *Learning to draw means learning to see the way artists do.* There are a few basic elements of shape that provide the information needed to re-create any image, whether simple or complex, on a piece of paper. (Be sure that students have their own individual copy of the shape chart at this time.) As you study the chart, notice that there are two families represented: The Straight Line Family and The Curved Line Family. It is important to familiarize yourself with these elements by using all of your senses to explore and recognize them in your environment.

The Straight Line Family

When you examine straight lines in the environment, they are usually attached to things. It is necessary to visually separate them so that they can be recognized. For example, a picture frame can be seen as four individual lines that have been connected. Discover straight lines in the stem of a flower, the leg of a chair, and the edge of a box. When you are inside a manmade structure, there are an infinite number of straight lines.

Many people think that a straight line can only be thin. Look at the chart and find a straight line that is wide enough to be considered a rectangle. Introduce other examples of wide straight lines such as a ruler, a sidewalk, a door, or even the silhouette of a tall office building. At what point does a line become a shape and vice versa?

An angle is made from two straight lines joined together at one point. Look at the chart to see how an angle can be very thin and narrow or very open

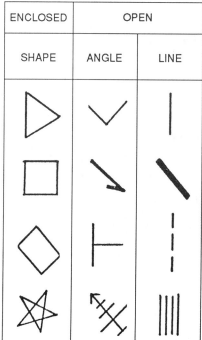

ENCLOSED	OPEN	
SHAPE	ANGLE	LINE

and wide. Think about how you can create triangles, rectangles, and squares when you join more than one angle line together. The corner of a book, the spokes on a bicycle, the bend in a ladybug's leg, and the point of a star are examples of angles that you can see everyday. The hands of a clock display a variety of angles as they move through a 12 hour period.

The Curved Line Family

As soon as a straight line begins to bend, it becomes a member of the curved line family. A line can bend in an infinite number of ways. Since curves have a tendency to be joined together in many different directions, it is important to isolate them so that they can be seen individually. The letter S, for instance, is really two curves fused together. A rainbow, the handle on a pitcher, a tree limb, the edge of a potato chip, and the contour of a banana are all examples of curved lines. As you look for curved lines in your environment, remember to notice the shapes on human beings. It will help prepare you to draw people.

When a curved line closes together, it becomes a shape. Challenge your vision to imagine as many different curved shapes as you can. The rim of a glass, a wedding ring, an egg, a braided rug, and a hot air balloon can be classified in this way. As you explore circular shapes in your environment, be aware that often we do not see the entire circle. When someone is wearing a ring on their finger, it is all but impossible to see the entire ring. Drawing ability is blocked when a person tries to draw what they are thinking about instead of what they actually see.

ENCLOSED	OPEN
SHAPE	LINE

4. *Getting to know both sides of your brain is an important step in learning to draw.* Your brain is approximately the size of a grapefruit and weighs about three pounds. It is the one organ we cannot transplant and still be ourselves. Seen from above, the human brain resembles the halves of a walnut—two similar appearing, rounded halves that are connected in the center. It is composed of two hemispheres, left and right, which are joined by the corpus callosum. The human nervous system is connected to the brain in a crossed-over fashion. The LH controls the right side of the body while the RH controls the left side.

    The cerebral hemispheres in the brains of animals are essentially alike, or symmetrical, in function. However, human cerebral hemispheres are organized asymmetrically in terms of function. The left hemisphere focuses on verbal, logical, analytical thinking. It excels in reading, writing, mathematics, and speech. The right half of the brain specializes in visual, spatial, perceptual information. It processes experience in a nonlinear and nonsequential fashion by looking at the whole, all at once. It seeks relationships between the parts and searches for a way to fit the parts together. Below is a list of functions which are generally attributed to the left and right hemispheres. Recent research indicates that there is a less clear division of functions between the hemispheres than was thought to be the case. Therefore, the terms L-Mode and R-Mode are often used because they designate a style of thinking that may or may not originate in a particular hemisphere of the brain.

L-Mode	R-Mode
verbal	nonverbal
linear	global
sequential	simultaneous
analytical	synthetic
logical	intuitive
symbolic	concrete

5. *Learning to draw requires learning to control mental shifts in brain mode.* During the 1950's, Dr. Roger Sperry conducted a series of animal studies in which the corpus callosum was severed. This connector, composed of 200 million fibers, provides a pathway for memory and learning between the two hemispheres. When Dr. Sperry severed the corpus callosum in the brains of cats and monkeys, the results were remarkable. There was no great change in the behavior of the animals. Their habits and coordination remained unchanged. However, when the animals were trained to specific tasks they were found to have two independent minds, each with its own kind of perception, memory, and decision system.

In the 1960's, similar operations were performed on a limited number of human patients suffering from intractable epilepsy. After all other remedies had failed, neurosurgeons Phillip Vogel and Joseph Bogen found a way to control these seizures by performing an operation that severed the corpus callosum, thus isolating one hemisphere from another. As a result, the patients' seizures were controlled and they regained health. Their outward appearance, manner, and coordination were little changed. But as in the case of the monkeys and cats, two separate minds could be determined.

Sperry and his associates devised a series of ingenious and subtle tests to find out what was happening in the two separated hemispheres. The tests provided evidence that each hemisphere perceives reality in its own way. The verbal half of the brain—the left mode—dominates most of the time in individuals with intact brains as well as in the split-brain patients. The right, subdominant half of the brain, also experiences the world but in a nonverbal, global way. In our own brains, with intact corpus callosa, communication between the two hemispheres combines these two perceptions and in doing so maintains our sense of being one, unified person.

Evidence found by Jerre Levy in her doctoral studies shows that the mode of processing used by the right brain is not only different from but also comparable in complexity to the left brain's verbal mode. In addition, Levy found that the two modes of processing sometimes seem to interfere with each other, thus preventing optimum performance. These findings are particularly significant for anyone who is interested in learning how to draw. The ability to draw appears to depend on whether you are able to "turn-off" the LM and "turn-on" the RM. The right brain processes visual information in such a way that artists can "see" the lines, shapes, and angles of the image they draw. The left brain cannot perceive visual information in this fashion although it often rushes in with words and symbols, trying to do a job for which it is not suited.

Since freehand drawing is largely a right-brain function, how can we keep the left-brain out of it? Split-brain studies indicate that the left-brain is not likely to allow the right-brain to take over unless it really dislikes the job. It is possible to "turn-off" the LM by introducing a task which it is unwilling or unable to do. The following exercise is designed to facilitate a mental shift from L-Mode to R-Mode. (Take a moment to do this exercise with students.) Have students close their eyes. Tell them to see the word cat written on a chalkboard. Now ask them to picture a cat chasing a butterfly in a meadow. Continue this exercise by introducing a variety of other simple words and corresponding images. Some individuals find it difficult to picture the cat or other images that are suggested during this exercise. However, with practice, the RM steps forward to do what the LM cannot. A mental shift can also be achieved by doing the mirror imaging exercises and upside-down drawings that are introduced in Quadrant III.

During drawing sessions, it is important to play music that can relax and quiet the mind. Music should be selected which has no driving beat or compelling melodic progression. Appropriate music will aid you in reaching a state conducive to RM concentration and visual focus. The following selections are recommended:

-Steve Halpern's *Anti-Frantic Alternative Music*, specifically "Comfort Zone," "Spectrum Suite," "Dawn," "Ancient Echoes," and "Star Born Suite"
-Harp music, such as Georgia Kelly's
-Flute music, such as Zamfir and Paul Horn's
-Pachelbel — Canon in D
-Go for Baroque — by RCA
-Bach — Mass in B minor
-Mozart —The Vespers

6. *Real artists draw from their imaginations and from filing cabinets full of pictures.* Professional artists decide what they want to draw, say a lion in the wild. So they study pictures of lions and they go to the zoo and study the movements and energy of lions. They use their imagination for style and composition. Then they begin making several sketches of lions. They also study a lot of data about the

Student artists should have the same options as the professionals. Yet many beginning artists believe they are cheating if they copy an idea or an image from a photograph or illustration. We need to understand that it is okay and is in fact very desirable to use all types of graphic materials for artistic inspiration. Begin collecting materials that will draw out the artist within you. Train your eyes to spot possible subjects on greeting cards, wrapping paper, coloring books, magazines, brochures, and posters. And remember to take snapshots, lots of them. You will draw more when you have more models to draw from. In freehand drawing, the integration of observation and imagination is essential.

Evaluation:

Objective quiz.

Freehand Drawing Quadrant III — How?

5. Left Mode — Working on Defined Concepts

Objectives:

To practice finding and identifying the Basic Elements of Shape.

To experience a mental shift from the L-Mode to the R-Mode through mirror image exercises and upside-down drawing.

Activities:

The activities in this step will help your students enrich their visual perception of the world and develop their drawing ability. Before your fledgling artists put pen to paper, take time to build their ability to "see" by playing some of the suggested visual games. Then move on to the mirror image exercises and the upside-down drawing.

When your students have had ample opportunities to do these warm-ups, they will be ready to draw the three-dimensional subjects described in step 8. If you are working with primary age children, you may wish to refer to Mona Brookes' book entitled *Drawing With Children.* In it she introduces many exercises and activities that work well with primary age children.

Play a Visual Game

An endless variety of games and exercises can be used to "see" the basic elements in their environment. You do not have to wait for a scheduled drawing time to play these games. Do them as a sponge activity whenever you have a few extra minutes. The following visual warm-ups can be used along with others that you and your students devise:

Call out one of the elements of shape and have a student find an example of it.

Collect a group of objects which combine two or more of the shape elements. Have students name every element that is represented in its makeup. A tape dispenser, a record player, and a globe would work well for this activity.

Ask students to work with a partner. Tell them to list all of the letters in the alphabet that have:

> -two or more angles
> -straight and curved lines
> -only curved lines

Manuscript letters work best for this exercise. Be sure to specify upper or lower case letters.

Display art prints and have students locate the basic shape elements within the print.

Mirror Image Drawing

Drawing two sides of an object that look the same but are in reverse order is a challenge that takes some practice. This is a skill your students will need when they draw vases or bottles and when they draw both sides of the body. Work through the steps below as you do this exercise with your class.

1. Make a class set of work sheets with three or four mirror image samples for students to complete. (See figure 1.) Also make an overhead transparency of the work sheet to help you introduce the exercise.

2. Distribute the work sheets. Begin by modeling the following procedure on the overhead or chalkboard. Show students how to trace over the line that appears on the left hand side of the first mirror image sample. As your overhead marker or chalk moves over the original line, have students name the type of lines and shapes they see. Then ask students to trace over the corresponding line on their work sheet.

3. Next start at the top of the first mirror image sample and show students how to draw the profile in reverse. Now it's their turn. Some students have difficulty drawing in the reverse. When this happens, point to the dotted line running down the center of the first sample. Ask them if they should draw their line toward or away from the dotted line in order to create the reversed direction.

   As students begin to draw in the reverse direction, they often experience a mental conflict. To achieve symmetry, it is necessary for them to become closely connected to the shapes and spaces. They may find themselves scanning back and forth in the space between the two lines, estimating inward-curving and outward-curving shapes. It becomes necessary for them to make continual adjustments in

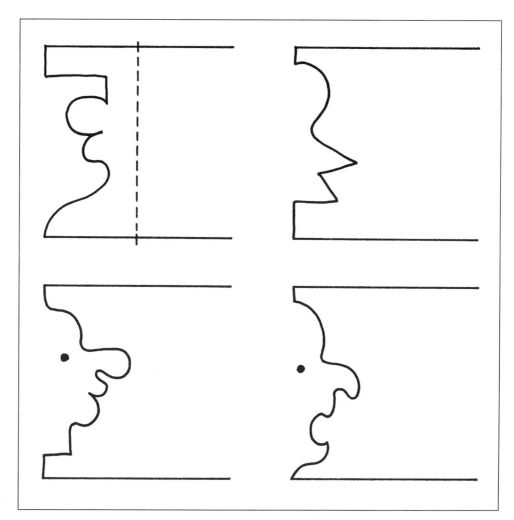

figure 1

the line they are drawing by checking where they have been and where they are going. Mirror-image drawings enable students to shift from the verbal, analytical mode to a spatial, nonverbal state. Students should learn to recognize and foster this state in themselves so that they can shift easily into it whenever they want to draw.

When you prepare mirror image warm-ups for children under 8-9 years old, make them very simple, with only one or two combinations of elements. Older students will enjoy doing the vase-face drawings found in Betty Edward's *Drawing On the Right Side of the Brain*. [13] Undoubtedly some of your students will want to create their own mirror image drawings to share with the class.

Upside-down Drawings

When a picture is in an upright position, we can recognize familiar things, name them, and classify them by matching what we see with our stored memories. However, when a picture is upside-down, familiar things do not look the same and the brain becomes confused. A person's own handwriting, turned upside-down, is difficult, if not impossible, to decipher. To test this, ask your students to find something they have written, and have them try to read it upside-down.

Provide students with an opportunity to do a series of upside-down drawings so that the R-Mode can continue to assert itself. The L-Mode will soon turn-off because this is not the kind of task it likes. Before you begin this task, read the following directions:

1.   Locate a series of simple line drawings similar to the kind you find in some coloring books. Make a collection of overhead transparencies from these drawings and organize them by their level of difficulty.

2.   Schedule a 20-30 minute block of time for drawing. Choose a very simple image, such as the bird in figure 2a. Place the image on the overhead upside-down. Dim the lights and play some background music to help students relax and focus. (Refer to the music selections suggested in Quadrant II.)

3.   Have students take a moment to study the upside-down drawing. Ask them to notice how all the lines fit together, where one line ends and another begins.

4.   It's time to draw! Pass out any type of 8 1/2 x 11 unlined paper. Students copy the upside-down image which means that their own drawing will also be upside-down. They should start at the top and copy each line. Tell them that although they may be able to recognize and name parts of the image, this should be avoided.The R-Mode needs to concentrate on lines and shapes in order to do do its job.

5.   When students finish, let them turn their drawings right side up and outline and/or color it with crayons and markers. Display them in the classroom.

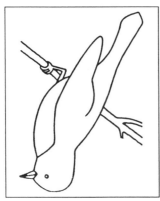

figure 2a   figure 2b   figure 2c
(Notice the increasing level of difficulty from 2a to 2c)

Evalutation:

How successful students are in turning-on the RM while completing the mirror image and upside-down drawings.

6. Right Mode — "Messing Around"

Objective:

To participate in four or more 3-dimensional drawing experiences which provide students with an opportunity to develop their own artistic style.

Activities:

In step 5, students become familiar with the R-Mode state by completing a series of mirror image exercises. They also practiced the general structure of objects by looking at 2-dimensional graphics. Now it is time for them to experience the challenge of drawing 3-dimensional subjects from the environment. In doing so, students will essentially use the same steps to accomplish drawing a 3-dimensional subject as they did in observing and drawing from 2-dimensional graphics. The main difference will be in training the eye to see the elements of shape on real subjects. In the first lesson, students will draw the simple collection of curved lines which form soft drink bottles. Shoes, kitchen gadgetry, tools, and plant life are other subjects they will draw in the lessons which follow. Be sure that students date and place all drawings in their portfolio *after* they have been displayed in the classroom.

#1 - The Soft Drink Bottle

What You Need:

Fine-tipped permanent black ink
  markers
A variety of soft drink bottles
Pencils with erasers
White drawing paper
Small container of very black cooled
  coffee
Watercolor brushes
Newspapers
Colored construction paper for
  making frames (optional)

What To Do:

1. One week before the lesson begins, ask students to bring in any
   type of soft drink bottles. You will
   need one bottle per student.

---

2. On the day of the lesson, designate one area of the room as a coffee-painting center. Lay down newspapers and provide containers of cooled coffee, small watercolor brushes, and a container of water for the cleaning of the brushes. (Make the coffee 3-4 times stronger than you would normally prepare it to drink.)

3. As the lesson begins, distribute the soft drink bottles among the students.

4. Ask students to close their eyes and feel the lines, ridges, and overall shape of the bottle. Discuss the experience.

5. Pass out sheets of white drawing paper and ask students to sketch the outline of the soft drink bottle with *their erasers*. If a student is not satisfied with the bottle she/he has sketched with the eraser, they can brush away the eraser crumbs and try again.

   Note: There are some students who prefer to use their pencil lead rather than the eraser. They are probably individuals who draw 3-dimensional objects with ease and do not require this transitional step. Allow them to start with their pencil lead.

6. When students are satisfied with the eraser outline, instruct them to draw over the eraser lines with their pencil lead. Then have them continue to draw the rest of the bottle with their pencil lead.

7. Have students trace over the lines of their soft drink bottle with a fine-tipped permanent black ink marker. Be sure to use permanent ink markers so the lines will not bleed when the bottles are painted with coffee.

8. Send small groups of students to the coffee-painting center. Ask them to fill their bottle with liquid refreshment by painting coffee inside their bottle.

9. When the painted drawings are dry, cut pieces of colored construction paper which can be used to frame each drawing.

10. Find an area of the classroom where you can display all of the bottles. No two soft drink bottles look alike and it is amazing how much each drawing reflects the personality of its artist. Already your students are developing an artistic style of their own.

    Note: This lesson can easily be extended by asking students to bring in other types of bottles, containers, and vases to sketch during another art period.

#2 - *Portrait of a Shoe*

What You Need:

Your shoes
Pencil

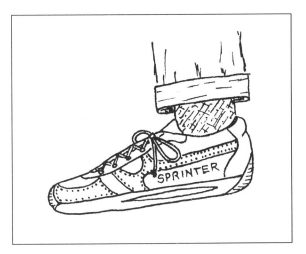

White drawing paper
Crayons or water color markers
Colored construction paper for frames
   (optional)

What To Do:

1. The day before this lesson, tell students to wear a pair of shoes that they would like to draw.

2. Instruct students to take off a shoe and examine it. Ask them to describe the shape of it and ask them to point out every detail they can.

3. Have students consider what view of the shoe they want to sketch. They might choose to draw their shoe from the side, front, back, or by looking down on it. Some might choose to draw more than one view.

4. Pass out white drawing paper and tell students to sketch their shoe. It is very helpful for students to use the pencil eraser to sketch the overall shape of the shoe. After that, the rest of the details fall into place quite easily.

5. When students have finished their drawings, ask them to use crayons or markers to color their shoe.

6. Make a frame of colored construction paper for each shoe and display them in the room.

#3 — All Manner of Gadgetry

What You Need

An assortment of kitchen utensils, garage tools, etc.
Pencils with erasers
White drawing paper
Fine-tipped permanent ink markers
Containers of cooled coffee
Watercolor brushes
Colored construction paper to make frames

What To Do:

1. Before the day of this lesson, ask students to help collect gadgetry.

2. When the collection is complete, share each object with the class and tell them they will be asked to draw one or more of the objects.

3. Pick out one of the objects and ask students how they would begin to draw it.

4. Distribute the gadgetry and drawing paper among the students. Remind students to close their eyes and feel the shape, lines, and texture of the object. Tell students they are welcome to begin their sketch with the eraser or with the pencil. Many students will have the confidence to skip the eraser step.

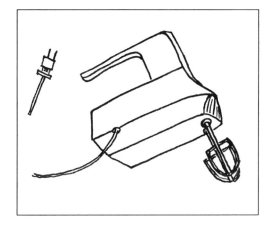

5. Have students trace over the lines of their object with a permanent marker.

6. Send small groups to the coffee-painting center. Instruct them to paint the surface of their object with coffee.

7. When the painted drawings are dry, cut pieces of colored construction paper which can be used to frame each drawing.

8. Display the gadgetry drawings in the classroom for everyone to observe and enjoy.

#4 — Leaves and Petals

What You Need:

Green plants, fresh and dried flowers
White drawing paper and scratch paper
Pencils with erasers
Crayons, colored chalk, or watercolor markers.

What To Do:

1. Bring a collection of leafy branches and place them in various parts of the classroom.

2. Discuss the leaf and stem structure of the branches.

3. Pass out scratch paper and ask students to practice drawing leaves. Tell students to consider the different angles of the leaves as they study the branch.

4. When individual students are ready, pass out white drawing paper and let them begin sketching the entire branch. Students could use crayons, chalk, or watercolor markers to give their drawing color.

5. On other days, bring in a collection of green plants, dried or fresh flowers. Give students opportunities to sketch these whenever time permits.

Evaluation:

The quality of student drawings. Sometimes students do not concentrate as they draw. This is evident in their completed work and I ask them to redo these drawings.

Freehand Drawing Quadrant IV —If?

7. *Left Mode — Analyzing their own application of the concepts for usefulness, originality, and as a stepping stone for future learning.*

Objectives:

To retake the Freehand Drawing Opinionnaire
To compare/contrast student responses on the first and second opinionnaire.
To have students plan the Still Life Masterpiece they will create.

Activities:

Provide each student with a copy of the Freehand Drawing Opinionnaire and ask them to take it for the second time. Explain that they will be comparing their responses on the first opinionnaire to the one they are now completing. When everyone is ready, again tally the class response to each statement on a bar graph. Then pass out the art portfolios. They contain the 1st opinionnaire and all assigned drawings—including the tree they drew from their imagination on the first day. Give students time to browse through these drawings and compare the results of their first and second opinionnaire.

Begin a discussion about the results of the opinionnaire by asking if anyone has changed their opinion about statement #1. Continue to discuss each of the five statements, encouraging students to share any personal experience during the unit which changed their original opinion about a particular statement. When everyone has had their say, show students the first and second bar graphs. Have them compare both graphs and point out general trends which have occurred during the course of this unit. You will probably hear students express many positive feelings about freehand drawing during the discussion. They may not be able to immediately draw every image they attempt but that is okay. Each drawing serves as a step toward the ones they end up liking. The variety of activities around the wheel have enabled students to see that drawing is a skill which can be practiced and perfected. Knowing this encourages students to continue drawing and learning and liberates them to find creative solutions to their drawing problems.

At this time students should begin to plan their final project—A Still Life Masterpiece. Still life means an arrangement of inanimate objects that are used for the purpose of drawing. The objects will need to be arranged in a pleasing way. Students then observe and draw it according to their own interpretation. It is a good idea to bring in several still life art prints. Talk about the subject, the composition, light and dark areas, changes in texture, and other contrasts students see in each print. Discuss how we can tell that one thing is in front of another when an artist overlaps shapes and objects. Also bring in three or more related objects to class that could be used as the subject for a still life drawing. Let students suggest a variety of ways these objects can be arranged for drawing.

Following this orientation, instruct students to begin their own Still Life Masterpiece by completing the planning work sheet below. Tell them to collect three or more real objects they will use to build their arrangement. The subject may be a favorite group of toys, sports equipment, stationery supplies, vegetables, art materials, or kitchen utensils. Charcoal, chalk, crayon, colored markers, or watercolor can be used to create a still life. Check over the completed planning work sheets before students begin work.

Still Life Masterpiece Plan

1. What is the title of your still life? _____

2. What objects will you use? _____

3. Make a pencil sketch of the still life you will draw on the back of this paper.

4. What art materials will you need to complete your still life?

    _____

Evaluation:

The quality of the discussion comparing the response to the first and second opinionnaire.

The completion of a planning worksheet by each student.

8. *Right Mode — Doing it themselves and sharing what they do with others*

    Objective:

    To draw a Still Life Masterpiece.

Activity:

Students draw Still Life Masterpieces based on their own selection and arrangement of objects. Create a construction paper frame for each still life and ask each student to share his/her masterpiece with the class. Then make arrangements to display these drawings in a local business or in a prominent location within the school. Students will be motivated to spend more time on these drawings when they know their work will be celebrated by the public eye.

Evaluation:

The successful completion and display of student Still Life Masterpieces.

Color

Can you imagine a world without color? Visualize yourself walking across damp gray grass while looking up into a black morning sky. Or think about the last time you watched a movie on a black and white television. The idea of living in a black and white world is certainly a dismal one. Yet we all tend to take color for granted because we experience it so effortlessly. As you continue reading, see if you can form a clear image of the colors described below:

> New blades of emerald green grass
> Ripe red cherries
> A soft blue robin's egg
> Delicate yellow wildflowers
> A bright orange popsicle

Color is one of the most exciting and stimulating sensations known to mankind. It can be an ongoing source of pleasure if we are willing to take a moment now and then to notice and enjoy it.

While color provides us with a tremendous source of pleasure, it also helps us to communicate. In sports, different colored uniforms designate different teams. Red, yellow, and green traffic lights govern the movement of traffic. Spaces and lines on maps are printed in different colors to help us understand important information about a particular geographical area. Blue may stand for rivers, green for parks and forests, and black for highways or roads. Color symbolizes our nation in the flag and announces holidays such as Christmas, Easter, and the 4th of July. It also provides clues about the seasons.

In the pink. . . feeling blue. . . green with envy. . . red with anger. . . rose-colored spectacles. . . a jaundiced view. . . and the list goes on. Phrases such as these are an integral part of our language because color is so strongly reflective of our feelings and thoughts. Furthermore, we are now realizing that color can directly affect our emotions, modifying our moods, actions, and even our health. Seventy years ago color was used very little in the everyday life of people in the United States. Today people select the colors of their clothing carefully and put much effort into decorating their homes and businesses with colors that create beautiful, restful, or exciting effects. In advertising, colors are selected which will appeal to the consumer, ultimately translating into a higher margin of profit. The white clothing of surgeons and their operating assistants is being traded in for the more soothing pastel shades of green and blue. It is to our advantage to learn all that we can about color so that it can be used to improve and enrich the quality of our daily lives.

When students study color, they need to make their own rainbow. Rainbows can be made with prisms, clear glasses filled with water, bubbles, or a spray of water from the garden hose. I often challenge students to see how many different ways they can make a rainbow. One year my class was amazed to discover that they could create a beautiful rainbow using a fishbowl full of water. Once students have created their own spectrum of color, they should be asked the following question —What is color?

So what is color? Color is a sensation produced by the action of the white light rays received by the retina of the eye. Although we speak of seeing colors or objects, we do not actually see them. Instead we see the light that objects reflect. While we look at an object, light coming from that object enters our eyes. Each eye focuses the light, forming an image of the object on the retina, a thin layer of tissue covering the back and sides of the inside of the eyeball and containing millions of light-sensitive cells. Most of the light that falls on the retina is absorbed and converted into electrical signals. These electrical signals then travel through nerves to the brain.

To understand what produces the color seen in their rainbow, students need to know something about the nature of light. Light is a form of radiant energy traveling through space in the form of waves. As it travels, it vibrates. The rate of vibration can be measured in units known as Angstrom units (A), measuring one-ten-millionth of a millimeter. The color red has a wavelength varying from 6200 to 6700 A; orange from 5900 to 6200; yellow from 5600 to 5900; green from 5100 to 5600; blue from 4700 to 5100; indigo from 4500 to 4700; and violet from 4000 to 4500. Light that contains all wavelengths in the same proportions as sunlight appears white.

When a beam of white light passes through a prism, the rays of different wavelengths are bent. The bending breaks the sunlight into a beautiful band of color which contains all the colors of the rainbow. At one end of the spectrum, the light appears as violet. It consists of the shortest wavelengths of light that we can see. As our vision travels from one end of the spectrum to the other, the light has increasingly longer wavelengths. It appears as blue, green, yellow, orange, and red, each one shading into its neighboring colors in the spectrum. The longest wavelengths of light appear to us as deep red in color.

Today manufacturers and artists create items in a tremendous variety of colors. To do so, they use one of two basic methods:

(1)   Mixing colorants
(2)   Mixing colored lights

Colorants are chemical substances that give color to such material as ink, paint, crayons, and chalk. Most colorants consist of fine powders that are mixed with liquids, wax, or other substances. Colorants that dissolve in liquids are called dyes. Colorants that do not dissolve but spread through liquids or other substances are called pigments.

When light strikes pigments in paint, the pigments absorb or subtract certain wavelengths of light at the same time that they reflect others. In paint containing a mixture of different pigments, each pigment subtracts different wavelengths. Because the color we see is the result of which wavelengths have been subtracted, creating colors by mixing pigments can be thought of as color by subtraction. For example, when paint with blue pigment is mixed with paint containing yellow pigment, the resulting paint appears green. Blue pigment absorbs virtually all of the light of long wavelengths (red, orange, and yellow) while yellow pigment absorbs most of the light of short wavelengths (blue and violet). Most of the light of medium wavelengths is not absorbed but reflected through the surface of the paint. As this light reaches our eyes, we see the paint as green. However, when lights of a different color are projected onto a screen, they blend together onto the screen and produce new colors by adding light of different wavelengths. For this reason, colored light mixtures are sometimes called color by addition.

After students understand the nature of light and color, it is important for them to have a way of thinking and talking about color. In 1898, an artist and teacher named Albert A. Munsell created a color chart system that not only allows us to see the colors of the spectrum but to use them for mixing, coordinating color schemes, etc. Hue, value, and intensity are three different dimensions that can be applied to each color. These qualities, discovered by a scientist name Helmholz, provide the foundation for the Munsell System.

Hue is the name of a color. It is as simple as that. Knowing the hue of colors allows us to distinguish one color from another by name. As students study and name the colors on a color wheel, they also need an opportunity to make a wheel of their own. They can be told that red, yellow, and blue are the primary colors from which all other colors are mixed. But they must discover this for themselves. The true challenge begins when students try to create one of the secondary colors. When red and blue are mixed together to make purple, everyone soon learns how difficult it is to mix the particular intensity of purple they are expecting to see. During this activity, you may hear students asking:

> "How many drops of blue and red?"

> "Why does everyone else's purple look so different from mine?"

> "Wouldn't it be easier to just paint the entire wheel with pre-mixed paints?"

I always smile when I hear these comments because learning to mix colors is not as easy as it looks. However, the increased understanding of color theory is well worth the effort students make.

Value is the lightness or darkness of a color. When we want to change the value of a particular color, white or black is added. Black and white are not colors. They do have value but lack hue and intensity. When mixing color, white is added to create a TINT of the color. We have lightened the value of the color but have not changed the hue. When adding black to a color, a SHADE of the color is obtained. Still, the hue has not been changed. Students can learn about changing the value of the color by making a color ladder similar to the color samples found in paint stores. In doing so, they will begin to understand why artists often change the value of a color they are using to achieve a particular effect in a painting.

Intensity refers to the purity or strength of a color. A color is brighter in its pure state than when mixed with any other color, black, white, or gray. Artists rarely use paints straight from the tube (in their strongest intensity). In mixing colors, there are many ways to change the intensity of a color but the two principal methods are:

1. Mixing a color with its complement.
2. Adding white, black, or gray.

When we study intensity, I set up a color lab in the back of the classroom. Students experiment with different methods of changing the intensity of a color. They find samples of colors whose intensities have been altered and then try to create the same color on their palettes.

Color is a subject which can be explored in great depth. I believe that it is important to spend as much time as we can acquainting ourselves and our students with this particular element. When we bring the study of color into the classroom, students learn to:

- Use color more creatively in art.

- Become more knowledgeable about selecting and arranging the colors they encounter in their daily environment.

- Communicate their ideas and feelings through color.

- Be more aware of color as a source of personal pleasure and joy.

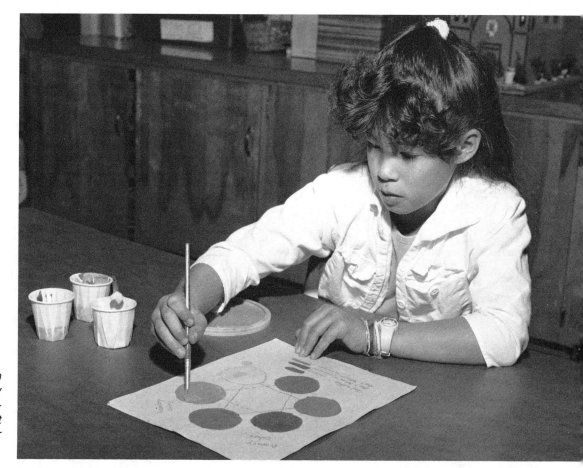

Concentrating on mixing secondary colors from the primary colors, a student works on her color wheel.

Color Color Color Color Color

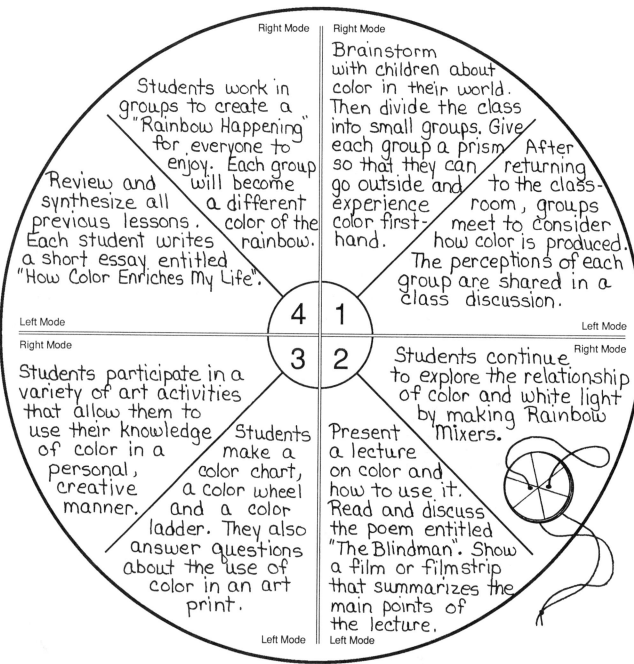

Right Mode (Quadrant 1)
Brainstorm with children about color in their world. Then divide the class into small groups. Give each group a prism so that they can go outside and experience color first-hand. After returning to the classroom, groups meet to consider how color is produced. The perceptions of each group are shared in a class discussion.

Right Mode (Quadrant 4)
Students work in groups to create a "Rainbow Happening" for everyone to enjoy. Each group will become a different color of the rainbow.

Left Mode (Quadrant 4)
Review and synthesize all previous lessons. Each student writes a short essay entitled "How Color Enriches My Life".

Left Mode (Quadrant 1)

Right Mode (Quadrant 2)
Students continue to explore the relationship of color and white light by making Rainbow Mixers.

Left Mode (Quadrant 2)
Present a lecture on color and how to use it. Read and discuss the poem entitled "The Blindman". Show a film or filmstrip that summarizes the main points of the lecture.

Right Mode (Quadrant 3)
Students participate in a variety of art activities that allow them to use their knowledge of color in a personal, creative manner.

Left Mode (Quadrant 3)
Students make a color chart, a color wheel and a color ladder. They also answer questions about the use of color in an art print.

Based on the 4MAT system model by Bernice McCarthy.

Color Quadrant I — Why?

1. Right Mode — Create an Experience

Objective:

To experience color by creating a spectrum of color with a prism.

Activity:

For several days prior to this unit, talk with students about many, many aspects of color in their lives: their favorite colors, how different colors make them feel, what it would be like to live in a black and white world. Then divide the class into small groups of 4 or 5. Give a prism and a sheet of unlined white paper to each group. Take the groups outside so that they can make their own rainbow on the paper. Clear glasses filled with water can be substituted for prisms.

Evaluation:

The success of each group in manipulating the prism to create a spectrum of color.

2. Left Mode — Analyze the Experience

Objective:

To analyze their experience with the prism by discussing a series of questions about color and light.

Activity:

All groups return to the classroom for a discussion. The following questions can be used to guide the discussion.

A. Were you able to create a spectrum of color with the prism?

B. How many different colors did you see? Name them.

C. What produces the colors you saw?

D. What is color?

E. Are there other ways to break white light into a spectrum of color? Make a list.

Evaluation:

The quality of students' contributions to the class discussion.

Color Quadrant II —What?

3. *Right Mode — Integrate Reflections into Concepts?*

    Objective:

    To enlarge student understanding of the relationship between white light and the colors of the spectrum.

    Activity:

    Make A Rainbow Mixer

    The first man to discover that ordinary white light is really a combination of bright colors was Sir Isaac Newton. While working on a telescope, he noticed that sunlight (white light) was broken into seven different colors of the spectrum —the same colors which we see in a rainbow. To prove his theory that white light contains all the colors of the spectrum, Newton projected these colors back through another prism. The result was white light again. The simple experiment described below enables students to test Newton's theory for themselves.

    What you need:

    Cardboard, white paper, glue, scissors, pencil, ruler, watercolor paints, and string.

    What you do:

    1. Cut a cardboard circle five inches wide. (See Figure 1.)

    2. Cut another circle the same size from the white paper. Paint the various sections of the circle according to Figure 2. Ordinary watercolors will serve quite well for this.

    3.   Allow time for the paint to dry. Glue the paper and cardboard circles together. Make two small holes near the center of the disk, about one inch apart. See Figure 1: "x" and "y."

    4. Thread about 4 feet of string through each hole. Tie the ends together as shown in Figure 3.

    5. Hold the string by the loops at each end and get a friend to slide the cardboard disk along until it is midway between your hands. Now twirl the disk around until the string is tightly twisted and pull gently

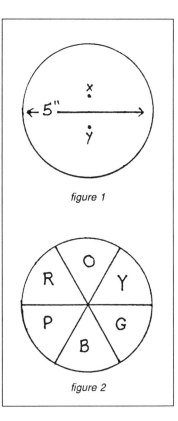

figure 1

figure 2

on the loops. You will soon find it quite easy to keep the disk spinning at high speed. (See Figure 4.)

6. Once the card is spinning around really fast you will find that the bright colors you have painted on it merge to produce a reflection that is almost white. If the colors were pure, they would turn pure white.

Evaluation:

The successful construction and operation of the "Rainbow Mixer."

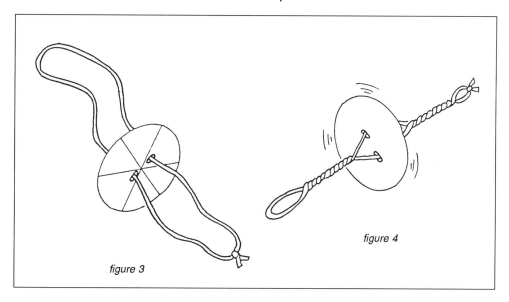

figure 3

figure 4

4. Left Mode — Develop Theories and Concepts

Objective:

To learn about color theory.

To learn how color is organized and used by artists.

To examine the psychological dimension of color.

Activity:

Give a lecture on color and how to use it. Before the lecture, display a collection of art prints that illustrate the various attributes of color. The following artists are noted for their use of color: Wayne Thiebaud, Auguste Renoir, Sam Francis, Vincent Van Gogh, Victor Vasarely, Claude Monet, Joseph Albers, Hans Hoffman, Marc Chagall, and Henri Matisse.

Refer to art prints often throughout the lecture. During your lecture, emphasize that color is one of the art elements and should be studied from the perspective of both science (the light spectrum) and art (the pigment system). The ten points listed below are important aspects of color and should be included in the lecture, depending on the age and background of the students. Be sure to read "The Blindman" by May Swenson and allow students to share their thoughts about this unusual piece. On the day following the lecture, show a film that examines the main points of the lecture.

1. Color is one of the art elements.

2. All color theory is based on the principle that color is light.

3. Color is a sensation produced by the action of white light rays received by the retina of the eye and interpreted by the brain.

4. The light spectrum results in white light when all of its components are mixed while the pigment spectrum produces a dark value approximating black.

5. Paint pigments are solid substances ranging from transparent to opaque. Each one has its own absorption and reflecting qualities.

6. Red, yellow, and blue are primary colors that can be mixed to obtain secondary colors. Tertiary colors are obtained by mixing a primary and a secondary color.

7. Hue, value, and intensity are important dimensions of color.

8. Color harmony can be achieved by using analogous, monochromatic, and/or complementary colors.

9. Color can be obtained from natural substances such as grass, berries, and walnut shells.

10. Emotional/sensual responses are created by color:

A few simple examples of emotional responses to color are as follows:

    Yellow —sunlight, warming, happiness, comfort

    Red —fire, heat, excitement, danger

    Blue — water, ice, coolness, calmness, sky, distance

    Green —foliage, nature, calm, quietness

Read the following poem to the students.

The Blindman

The blindman placed
A tulip on his tongue for purple's taste
Cheek to grass, his green

Was rough excitement's sheen
of little whips
In water to his lips

he named the sea blue and white,
the basin of his tears and fallen beads of sight
He said: This scarf is red;

I feel the vectors to its thread
that dance down from the sun. I know
the seven fragrances of the rainbow.

I have caressed
the orange hair of flames. Pressed
to my ear,

a pomegranate lets me hear
crimson's flute.
Trumpets tell me yellow. Only ebony is mute.

By May Swenson

Evaluation:

Objective quiz

Color Quadrant III —How?

5. Left Mode — Working on Defined Concepts

Objective:

To review the language and organization of color by making a color chart.

To practice mixing, shading, and tinting colors by making a color wheel and a color ladder.

To apply what they have learned about color by writing about the use of color in an art print.

Activity:

This step on the wheel will take three class periods to complete. During the first period, students make a color chart as they follow a sequence of directions given by the teacher. During the second period, students make their own color wheel by mixing primary colors. They will also practice shading and tinting color by making a color ladder. The third period will provide students with an opportunity to apply what they have learned about color by writing about the use of color in an art print.

Making a Color Chart

What You Need:

White paper (9x12 or 12x18)
Crayons

What To Do:

Have students fold their paper to make 8 sections. See Figure 5. Number the sections as illustrated. Then give your students the following directions as you model each step on a large piece of paper, the chalkboard, or the overhead.

1.	2.	3.	4.
5.	6.	7.	8.

figure 5

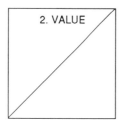

1. Label box #1 "Hue." Hue means the name of the color. Make a sample of red, yellow, blue, green, orange, and purple. Then write the name of each color beside the sample.

2. Value is the lightness or darkness of a color. In box #2 draw a diagonal line. Label the box "Value." Choose one color. Color in the upper section lightly. Make the color in the lower section dark.

3. Intensity is the brightness or dullness of a color. Label box #3 "Intensity" and divide the box by making a diagonal line. Color both sections of the box red. Now take a green crayon and color over the red in the upper section. The color in the lower section has greater intensity—it is brighter.

4. Colors can be divided into warm and cool colors. In box #4 list the warm colors and put a sample beside the word.

```
┌─────────────────────┐
│   5. COOL COLORS    │
│                     │
│   □ BLUE            │
│                     │
│   □ GREEN           │
│                     │
│   □ PURPLE          │
└─────────────────────┘
```

5. Label box #5 "Cool Colors." Write the colors and make a sample color beside each one.

```
┌─────────────────────┐
│    6. PRIMARY       │
│      COLORS         │
│                     │
│   □ RED            │
│                     │
│   □ YELLOW         │
│                     │
│   □ BLUE           │
└─────────────────────┘
```

6. Label box #6 on your paper "Primary Colors," then write down the primary colors and make a sample beside each word.

```
┌─────────────────────┐
│   7. SECONDARY      │
│      COLORS         │
│                     │
│  □ + □ = GREEN      │
│                     │
│  □ + □ = ORANGE     │
│                     │
│  □ + □ = PURPLE     │
└─────────────────────┘
```

7. Secondary Colors are obtained by mixing two primary colors. The secondary colors are orange (yellow + red), green (yellow + blue) and purple (blue + red). Label box #7 "Secondary Colors" and make two samples beside each word as you see in the illustration.

```
┌─────────────────────┐
│ 8. COMPLEMENTARY    │
│      COLORS         │
│       P.   S.       │
│  1.  □  -  □        │
│                     │
│  2.  □  -  □        │
│                     │
│  3.  □  -  □        │
└─────────────────────┘
```

8. Each primary color has a secondary color directly opposite it on the color wheel. These color pairs are known as complementary colors. Label box #8 "Complementary Colors" and color the samples for each complementary pair.

* Colors may be obtained from paints, crayons, and chalk. They may also be found in nature. Certain vegetable juices are colorful as are colors made from barks, berries, chocolate, coffee, and grass. You may wish to place a variety of these materials at a table and invite students to visit this "color center" so that they can make samples of these colors on a separate sheet of absorbent paper. Or provide your students with paper and let them work with natural colors found in their own kitchens and backyards.

Make a Color Wheel

What You Need:

1. A class set of color wheel outlines printed on 9x12 manila paper.
2. Red, yellow and blue tempera.
3. One paper plate per student.
4. Small containers of water and towels.

What To Do:

1. Before the lesson begins, squeeze 2 tsp. each of red, yellow and blue tempera on each paper plate and fill a small container of water for every student. Then place a color wheel outline, a paper plate with tempera, two brushes, a small container of water, and three paper towels on every student's desk.

2. Tell students to paint the red, yellow and blue circles on the color wheel work sheet using the paint on their paper plate.

3. Show students how to make a secondary color by mixing two primary colors. Now let them mix their own secondary colors on the paper plates so they can finish painting their color wheel.

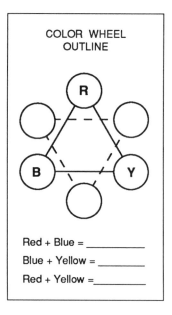

COLOR WHEEL OUTLINE

Red + Blue = _____
Blue + Yellow = _____
Red + Yellow = _____

Make a Color Ladder

What You Need:

| TINT # 4 |
| TINT # 3 |
| TINT # 2 |
| TINT #1 |
| BASIC COLOR |
| SHADE # 1 |
| SHADE # 2 |
| SHADE # 3 |
| SHADE # 4 |

Figure 6

1. A class set of color ladder outlines (Figure 6) printed on manila paper. (Actual size of the outline is 3-1/2x11.)
2. Paper plates for mixing paint.
3. Two small brushes per student.
4. Tempera paint in black, white and one basic primary or secondary color.
5. Small containers of water and paper towels.

What To Do:

1. Before the lesson begins, squeeze 2 tbsp. of tempera onto side A of the paper plate. Then squeeze two more tbsp. onto side B of the plate as shown in Figure 6. Next squeeze about 1 tsp. of white and 1 tsp. of black tempera on the same plate as shown. Provide each student with a color ladder outline, two paintbrushes, a container of water, and a paper plate which holds the tempera paint.

2. Direct students to paint some of the basic color from their paper palette onto the section of the color ladder labeled "Basic Color."

3. Instruct students to dip a clean brush into the white tempera, dropping a drop or two of it into the "basic color" on side A. The drop of white tempera and the basic color should be thoroughly mixed

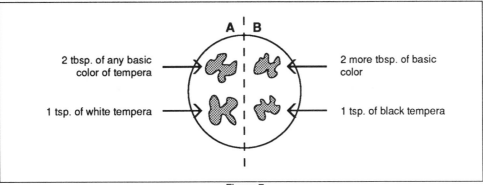

Figure 7

with a brush. Students then paint this tinted mixture onto the section of the ladder entitled tint #1.

4. Students continue to add one or two drops of white to the "Basic Color" before painting tint #2, tint #3, and tint #4.

5. Using the basic color and the black tempera on side B, repeat the procedure outlined in steps 3 and 4 as students paint in the sections labeled shade #1, shade #2, shade #3, and shade #4.

    Note: Students have a tendency to add a little too much white or black when they first begin shading and tinting the basic color.

Write About Color

Give your students an opportunity to apply what they have learned by writing about the color they see in a well-known art print. Choose an art print that illustrates characteristics of color with which students are familiar. Some or all of the following questions can be addressed by students as they study a particular print.

1. What colors do you see?
2. Are these colors warm or cool, light or dark, bright or dull?
3. What relationship do the colors have to each other? (analogous, complementary, monochromatic)
4. How is color used in terms of one or more of the following design principles?

    Perspective   Balance
    Contrast   Directional Movement
    Repetition   Positive/Negative
    Space

5. What mood does the color in this picture express?

6. Is color used symbolically?

Evaluation:

The quality of work on the completed color charts, color wheels, color ladders, and written responses to the questions about the art prints.

6. Right Mode — "Messing Around"

Objective:

The student will participate in three activities which give them an opportunity to use color creatively.

Activities:

The following art experiences are particularly appropriate for the intermediate and middle grades. It is a good idea to do each activity yourself so that you will know the procedure well.

Hand Me Some Color

What You Need:

An assortment of 9x12 con-
    struction paper
Glue
Scissors
Pencils

What To Do:

1. In preparation, create a striking multi-colored dis-
    play of construction paper on a table. Be sure that each student has a pencil, glue, and scissors.

2. Begin this activity by holding a discussion centered around the rich variety of colored construction paper on the table. Hold up two different colors of the construction paper at one time and discuss the effect one color has on another. Ask students to share their ideas about pleasing color combinations. Using samples of the construction paper, ask students to suggest color combinations that do not work. Invariably one student will dislike a particular color combination that another student especially likes. This difference in opinion is wonderful because it enables the class to appreciate the importance of individual taste in selecting and using color.

3. Show your students the "Hand Me Some Color" sample you have created. Discuss your own use of color.

4. Allow students to go to the table and select four sheets of construction paper. One sheet will be used for the background and the other three sheets will be used to make handshapes. You may want to impose a time limit for each group as they approach the table to select paper. Many students are intrigued by the variety of possible color combinations and could easily spend a great deal of time holding one color next to another.

5. When students have selected their construction paper, instruct them to lay one hand down on a piece of the paper and trace around it with a pencil. Students should then cut out that handshape and use it as a pattern to make the other two handshapes.

6. The handshapes should be arranged on the piece of construction paper that has been reserved for the background. The handshapes can be folded in various places to achieve a 3-dimensional effect. When students are satisfied with their arrangement, it's time to glue each piece into place.

7. The handshapes can be decorated with rings, freckles, bracelets nail polish, and colorful designs.

    Note: This activity can be completed on 12 x 18 paper using more handshapes.

Watercolor a Clown

What You Need:

Pictures of clowns
Pencil
White 12x18 drawing paper
Water color paints and brushes
Individual containers of water

What To Do:

1. Before this lesson begins, display a variety of clown portraits and provide each student with paper, paint, a brush, and water.

2. Tell your students that they will be drawing clown faces. Show them several pictures of clowns and discuss the colors and techniques used to create a "clown look."

3. Ask students to think about the shape they will draw for the clown's face. Will it be round, oval, or square?

4. Tell students that people's eyes are in the middle of the head. Some may want to measure with their hands to see that it is really so.

5. Students are now ready to lightly sketch the clowns. When they have finished, it is time to paint their clown and give it a name.

6. Display all the clowns and enjoy!

Clearly Colorful Chalk Drawings

What You Need:

9x12 or 12x18 manila, white, or black construction paper
A bowl of liquid starch and three, two inch brushes
A box of pastel chalk for each student
Pencil
Newspapers

What To Do:

1. In preparation, provide each student with a sheet of paper, a box of pastel chalk, and newspaper to cover the desk. Make a work area near the sink where students can go to brush liquid starch on their paper.

2. Students lightly sketch a picture on their paper. They might want to try making large flowers, insects, fish, geometric shapes, or a landscape scene from this planet or another.

3. When students finish their sketch, they go to the work area and brush about 3 tbsp. of liquid starch across the surface of their paper. They need to make sure the edges are covered and the starch is evenly spread over the paper.

4. Students return to their desks and draw with the chalk. They need to work quickly, for when the starch dries it will be difficult to move the chalk across the paper.

5. The starch will act as a fixative but you may wish to spray the dry pictures with a chalk fixative or hair spray to be sure the chalk does not rub off.

Evaluation:

How well students followed directions and used color to express their ideas.

7. *Left Mode — analyzing their own application of the concepts for usefulness, origninality and as a stepping stone for future learning.*

Objective:

To review what they have learned about color

To address their own thoughts and feelings about color by writing a short essay

To begin planning and organizing the "Rainbow Happening."

Activity:

The following activities require students to synthesize what they have learned about color.

1. Students share what they have learned about color in a class discussion. Their art work from Quadrant III is on display so that they can refer to it. After the discussion, students write a one page essay entitled "How Color Enriches My Life." Students exchange their essays with a partner so that they can read and share each other's ideas. Some of the essays are read to the entire class.

2. Students plan and organize the "Rainbow Happening." See Step 8 for more details.

Evaluation:

How well students shared and synthesized their ideas about color in the discussion and in the essay.

8. *Right Mode — Doing it themselves and sharing what they do with others*

Objective:

To participate in a "Rainbow Happening."

Acitivity:

Students work in six small groups to plan and organize a "Rainbow Happening." Each group selects one color of the rainbow until every color is represented. Once the color selection has been made, each group is asked to complete three or more of the seven color tasks listed below. Color task #1 is required of every group.

1. Collect a minimum of ten items in your group's color. These items will be used to create a monochromatic color display. Decide how

the items will be displayed and who will be the spokesperson when the display is shared. The spokesperson will share each item in the display and will then answer the following questions:

a. Which item in your display has the most intense color?
b. Which items are tints of _____?
c. Which items are shades of _____?

Note: This activity is so colorful that you will want to bring your camera. The individual displays combine to create a remarkable rainbow in your classroom.

2. On a large sheet of butcher paper, make a mind map of your color. Then use the ideas contained in the mind map to write a poem. The poem and perhaps even the mind map are shared with the class.

3. Find a tape or record that is "blue," "red," or whatever your assigned color is. Play this piece of music for the class and discuss why you selected it as a metaphor for your color.

4. All group members dress in the group color on the day of the "Rainbow Happening."

5. Bring a color coordinated snack for your classmates to enjoy. Orange carrot sticks, red strawberries, blue blueberry muffins, or green grapes can enhance a color presentation considerably.

6. Create a large poster that advertises your color. Write a slogan and draw images that show your color in its best light.

7. Create your own color idea to share.

On the day of the "Rainbow Happening," each group is given 10 minutes to set up its display. Arrange the display centers around the room according to the pattern of the rainbow. In turn, each group shares the three color tasks which it has completed. After all groups have shared, each group is invited to put one of the items from their monochromatic color display into the middle of another group's display. A red object placed in the middle of a monochromatic yellow display can cause quite a stir. When all groups have had an opportunity to place one of their items in another group's display, students should consider the role that contrasting colors play in our society. The teacher will want to invite students to bring in brightly colored cereal boxes and other products wrapped in contrasting colors. As students consider the role that colors play in selling products, it may be time to go around the wheel again.

Evaluation:

The quality of group work on each of the color tasks.

Shape/Form

You bring home a bagful of shapes every time you visit the grocery store. Mushrooms, carrots, peanuts and pasta are some of the foods that have their own shape. Children love to play with shapes. Squares and circles soon become a part of their visual memory as do hearts, clouds, and ice cream cones. It is quite possible to recognize a tree or an automobile from its shape alone. In fact, we all continue to identify and attach meaning to the many shapes we encounter throughout our lives.

Shapes can be defined as a line that has come home. In other words, a line that encloses an area creates a shape. But shapes can also be made without lines. For example, a shape is formed when you walk on a floor with wet feet or spill a little pancake batter on the stove. An artist can create shapes by drawing them in line and then filling them with color. Shapes can also be made by painting them on paper. In order to be a shape, it needs an edge. No matter how irregular or indistinct, it must have an edge to separate it from what it is not.

There are two families of shapes: geometric and free form. After exploring the difference between these two families, I often ask students to work with a partner and list as many examples as possible of each family. Partners soon find that they have found many examples of geometric shapes but very few items that are free form in shape. When the work period has ended, I ask, "Why

Shape/Form *Shape/Form*

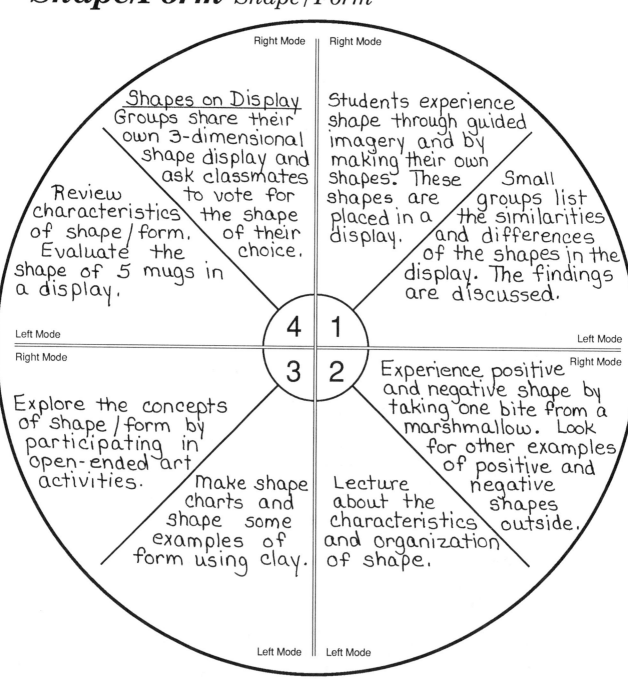

Right Mode | Right Mode

Shapes on Display
Groups share their own 3-dimensional shape display and ask classmates to vote for the shape of their choice.

Review characteristics of shape/form. Evaluate the shape of 5 mugs in a display.

Students experience shape through guided imagery and by making their own shapes. These shapes are placed in a display.

Small groups list the similarities and differences of the shapes in the display. The findings are discussed.

4   1

Left Mode | Left Mode

3   2

Right Mode | Right Mode

Explore the concepts of shape/form by participating in open-ended art activities.

Make shape charts and shape some examples of form using clay.

Lecture about the characteristics and organization of shape.

Experience positive and negative shape by taking one bite from a marshmallow. Look for other examples of positive and negative shapes outside.

Left Mode | Left Mode

Based on the 4MAT system model by Bernice McCarthy.

was it so difficult to list free form shapes?" This is not an easy question for them to answer. After some soul searching and a little teacher guidance, they realize that the most prevalent shapes in the manmade world are geometric while the most common shapes in nature are organic or free-form. Most of us are more familiar with the multitude of manmade shapes we see and use everyday. Our classroom and homes are filled with geometric shape. Following this discussion, I often challenge students to bring in as many examples of free-form shape as they can locate.

Form is a shape translated into volume. A child once told me that a circle is like a flat balloon. When the balloon is filled with air, the circle becomes a sphere. Although this is not a perfect analogy, it is a way to help children understand the difference between shape and form. A rectangle becomes a box or cylinder; a triangle—a cone or pyramid; an oval—an egg. Primary age children benefit from working with clay to create some or all of the forms listed above. Older students are challenged by an opportunity to combine two or more forms into an original sculpture. After children have shaped their own forms, it is time to investigate how form can be created on a two dimensional surface. Bring in lots of art prints. Study the way in which artists have used two dimensional shape to give an impression of depth and form in trees, city buildings, people, etc. Then ask students to draw or paint some of their own pictures using these techniques.

The artist knows that human beings respond to shapes visually. We get feelings and thoughts just from looking at combinations of shapes. Perhaps we have these ideas about shape because we are reminded of objects we have seen or because of the qualities of the shapes themselves. Whatever the reason, shape and form have a significant influence on our lives.

Shape/Form Quadrant I — Why?

1. Right Mode — Create an Experience

Objective:

Students will experience shape through guided imagery and by making a shape of their own.

Activity:

Share the following guided imagery with your students. Before you begin reading this section, ask students to make themselves very comfortable as they close their eyes and breathe deeply three times.

Shape is everywhere. It can be seen when you reach for a slice of pizza or pick up a shell at the beach. City buildings, mountains, ships at sea, and billowy clouds all have their own distinctive shape. We could say that shape is the result of a line that encloses a flat surface. Imagine that you are holding a string. Lay the string on the flat surface. Now make a shape by enclosing some of the surface with your string. Look at the shape you have just created. Is it made of curved lines, straight lines, or some of both? Perhaps this shape reminds you of a familiar object. . . As you continue studying your shape, choose a color that is right for it. Pick up a paintbrush and paint your shape this color.

Shapes can also be made without lines. Imagine that you are playing in the snow. One of your friends is chasing you down a hill. While running, you look back to see if your friend is coming. That is when you notice your perfectly formed footprints in the snow, shapes that were formed at once as you played.

Now see yourself walking in the park. The sun is setting. Everyone has gone home. It is so peaceful. You can almost hear the quiet. Yet it seems as if someone is walking with you. The someone is your shadow. For a moment you stand still, looking at the familiar shape that is your own silhouette. There are many other silhouetted shapes in the park. The picnic tables, a slide, some swings, and a cluster of pine trees all lay down their shadowy shapes as the day slips by.

An artist can create shapes by drawing them in line and then filling them in with color. This is what happened when you outlined a shape with string and painted it. But artists can also create a shape directly with a brush by using the brush to create the area and the boundaries of the shape at the same time. As you continue your day, notice and enjoy the wide array of shapes that surround you. Perhaps you will be surprised to see how many different shapes are a part of your everyday life.

At the conclusion of the guided imagery, provide students with a piece of 9x12 black paper and a pair of scissors. Tell the class that everyone will now have an opportunity to make their own shape. First, students use their pencil eraser to outline a shape on the black paper. Students may brush away the eraser crumbs and create a different shape if they are not pleased with their first attempt. Students who wish to make geometric shapes will want to use a ruler. After a shape has been outlined with an eraser, it should be outlined in pencil and cut out with a pair of scissors. All shapes are then mounted on a white background for everyone to enjoy.

Evaluation:

The quality of the completed shape display.

2. Left Mode — Analyze the Difference

Objective:

To reflect on the characteristics of shape by discussing the similarities and differences of the shapes in the display.

Activity:

Give the class an opportunity to look carefully at all of the student-made shapes. Ask the students to generate some shapes. Write these words on the board. Now divide the class into small groups. Instruct each group to list as many differences and similarities of the displayed shapes as they can find. When the groups have completed this task, discuss the findings of each group.

Evaluation:

The quality of students' contribution to the group lists and class discussion.

Shape/Form Quadrant II —What?

3. Right Mode — Integrate Reflections into Concepts

Objective:

To see and experience shapes made by positive and negative space.

Activity:

Give one marshmallow to each student with instructions not to eat it yet! Tell students to examine their marshmallow closely. Then ask, "How is the shape you made from construction paper different from your marshmallow?" Students will probably notice that a marshmallow is 3-dimensional and is made up of more than one shape. When all have become well acquainted with their marshmallow, direct them to take one bite without eating all of it. Discuss the positive shape of the partially eaten marshmallow and the negative shape created when the bite was removed. Take your class for a shape walk outside so they can look for other examples of positive and negative shape. Example: One cloud in a clear sky is a shape, but all of the sky around the cloud is a shape as well. You may wish to provide students with a piece of paper and pencil so they can draw the negative shape which surrounds a positive shape.

Evaluation:

Were students able to find other examples of positive and negative shape during the walk outside?

4. Left Mode — Develop Theories and Concepts

Objective:

To provide a formal definition of shape.

To become knowledgeable about the kinds, characteristics, and organization of shape and form.

To become acquainted with the expressive use of shape and form.

Activity:

Give a lecture on shape. Before the lecture begins, display a collection of art prints that illustrate the various attributes of shape. The following artists are well known for their use of shape: Mies Vander Rohe, M. C. Escher, Charles and Ray Eames, Ikko Tanaka, Henry Moore, Paul Klee, and Piet Mondrian. Include some or all of the following shape concepts in your lecture.

1. Definition of shape
   Areas that are enclosed by a line or the outside contours of a form. Shape can also be defined by color, value, or texture.

2. Kinds of shape
   Natural: Shapes that are found naturally in the environment.
   Man Made: Shapes that are constructed or invented by man.
   Geometric: Simple shapes created by laws of geometry. These shapes include a circle, triangle, rectangle, and other polygons.
   Free Form: Free constructed, unmeasured shapes.

3. Characteristics of shape
   a. Shapes used in the graphic arts are flat, 2-dimensional shapes.
   b. Shapes can also be 3-dimensional and have actual volume or thickness. Three-dimensional shapes are usually referred to as forms.
   c. Angular shapes are made up of straight lines such as rectangles, squares, triangles, or other polygons.
   d. Circular shapes are defined by curved, encircling lines such as an oval, crescent arc, semi-circle, or spiral.
   e. Shapes can be symmetrical or asymmetrical.

4. Organization of shape
   a. Shapes close together but not touching give a feeling of unity and togetherness.
   b. Overlapping shapes give a closed-in feeling and a feeling of depth.
   c. Shapes placed at the top of a page appear to descend, whereas shapes at the bottom of a page appear to ascend.
   d. Shapes can be arranged in a rhythmic or random manner to make patterns. Patterns can appear static to the eye or they can create an optical illusion of motion.

5. Design Principles
   Shape can be used to provide contrast, directional eye movement, balance, repetition, positive and negative space, and dominance in a work of art.

6. Expressive Use of Shape
   a. Decorative: Shapes can be used to ornament a composition.
   b. Representational: Shapes can be used to represent actual objects.

    c. Symbolic: Shapes can be used as symbols for ideas, concepts, things, or places such as flag symbols or religious symbols.
    d. Emotional: Shapes can depict emotional responses: happy, sad, restful, uplifting, fearful, etc.

There are many available films about shape and form. You may wish to show one of the films on the day following your lecture.

Evaluation:

Objective quiz

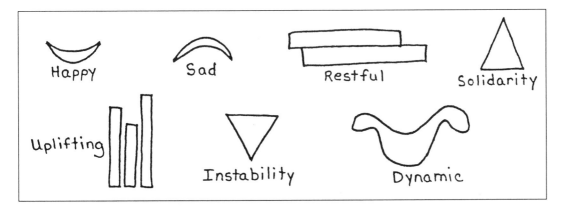

Shape/Form Quadrant III — How?

5. Left Mode — Working on Defined Concepts

Objective:

Students will create a shape chart and shape some examples of form using clay.

Activity:

Making a Shape Chart and Shaping Forms are both teacher directed exercises. Be sure to model and give precise directions as you proceed.

Making a Shape Chart

What To Do:

Provide each student with a sheet of paper and crayons or markers. Students fold their paper to make 8 parts as shown Figure 1. The boxes are numbered from one to eight. Give the following directions as students work to complete the chart.

1. Shapes are areas that are enclosed by a line or the outside contours of a form. Shape can be as simple as a circle or as complex as a piece of lace. In box #1, draw a shape and color it in.

1.	2.	3.	4.
5.	6.	7.	8.

figure 1

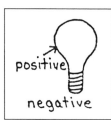

2. Shapes may be positive or negative. Point to the shape in box #1. The darkened area is the positive shape and the white area is the negative shape. In box #2 draw another shape and color it. Label the shape positive and the white outside area negative.

3. Shape may be free form or geometric. Draw one or more geometric shapes in box #3.

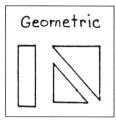

4. Draw a free form shape in box #4. See how many examples of free form shape you can find inside or outside the classroom.

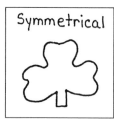

5. Some shapes are symmetrical, while others are asymmetrical. Make an example of one symmetrical shape in box #5.

6. Artists often place one shape in front of another. In box #6, make an example of overlapping shapes.

BEYOND WORDS

7. There can be shapes inside of shapes. In box #7 draw a shape, then draw another shape inside of the first one.

8. Shapes may be added to. Draw a shape in box #8 that resembles a city building. Now add one or more buildings to box #8. You may wish to add some doors and windows by putting a shape inside a shape.

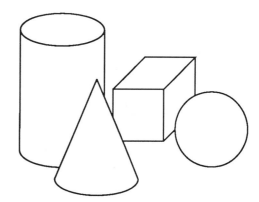

Shaping Forms. . .
a manipulative exercise

What You Need:

Modeling Clay
Newspaper
Wax Paper

What To Do:

1. Cover all student work areas with a pad of newspaper and a sheet of wax paper. Provide each student with a stick of modeling clay. Other types of clay can also be used.

2. Demonstrate how to shape the following forms out of modeling clay: a cylinder, a cube, a sphere, and a cone.

3. Have students mold the clay to make one example of each form. As students are working, ask them to name familiar objects that are made of cylinders, spheres, cubes, and cones.

4. Following the hands-on experience with clay, have the class look at prints or slides of sculptures and other objects that are made of simple forms. Ask students to name what forms the artist has used.

Related activity: Students combine two or more forms to make their own original sculpture.

Evaluation:

The quality of work on the completed shape charts and clay forms.

6. Right Mode — "Messing Around"

Objective:

To participate in four activities which give students an opportunity to use shape and form creatively.

Activities:

Each of the following art experiences focuses on one particular aspect of shape. In the 1st activity, Geometric Patterns, students create a design using one geometric shape that is repeated across the paper in various sizes. Your students will enjoy working with just one shape. Many interesting effects are created as they unconsciously strive to create a sense of balance and unity. Art activity #2 gives students an opportunity to make a visual statement through the use of positive and negative shape. This art experience represents a greater creative challenge for most students. Students will be more successful if you have several samples to show them before they start to work. "Newspaper Cities" is the title of the third art experience. Many students love the glamour and visual interest of a big city. They remember the shapes of city structures and have little difficulty cutting buildings of all sizes and shapes from a piece of newspaper. In the last activity, Box Towers, students work with 3-dimensional shapes. Each tower is usually constructed and collapsed numerous times until the builders are satisfied and ready to glue the pieces into place.

Geometric Patterns

What You Need:

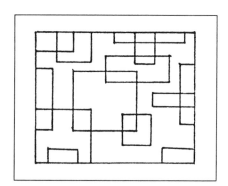

9x12 white paper
A black crayon
Watercolor paints and brush
Container of water
Paper towels

What To Do:

1. Distribute the necessary materials to everyone.

2. Tell students to select one geometric shape, such as a square, circle, or triangle, and using the black crayon, draw that shape on the paper. Repeat it all over the paper in various sizes. Press heavily so the lines are thick and dark.

3. Paint the shapes with watercolors, using many colors.

4. Let it dry thoroughly and mount on construction paper of a complementary color.

Positive and Negative Shapes

What You Need:

4-1/2x6 colored construction paper
9x12 colored construction paper
Scissors
Glue
Pencils

What To Do:

1. Distribute materials.

2. Tell students to draw shapes along the edges of a 4-1/2x6 sheet of colored construction paper.

3. Cut shapes from along the inside of the borders. Lay the design on a 9x12 sheet of contrasting paper.

4. Paste the shapes outside the borders to look as if each had simply been folded back from its original position. No extra paper is added or taken away from the original rectangle.

   Note: A colorful page from a wallpaper book or from a magazine may be substituted for the 4-1/2x6 sheet of colored construction paper.

Newspaper Cities

What You Need:

9x12 or 12x18 light blue construction paper
Pieces of the classified section of the newspaper
Small containers of liquid starch
Colored chalk
Scissors and paint brush

What To Do:

1. Distribute materials. Tell students to cut buildings of all sizes and shapes from a piece of newspaper. (The classified section works the best.)

2. Using the paint brush, cover the blue construction paper with

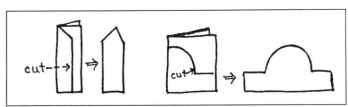

---

liquid starch. Lay the buildings on, one at a time, and cover each with the liquid starch.

3. Give the entire picture one last coat of starch and then add details such as windows, chimneys, etc., with colored chalk.

Box Towers

What You Need:

Boxes with lids
Tempera paint
Brushes
Paint
Glue
Newspapers

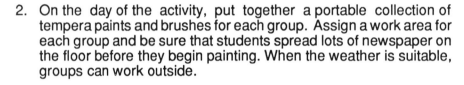

What To Do:

1. One week before this activity, form small groups of students. Ask each group to collect a wide assortment of boxes to be used for constructing a box tower.

2. On the day of the activity, put together a portable collection of tempera paints and brushes for each group. Assign a work area for each group and be sure that students spread lots of newspaper on the floor before they begin painting. When the weather is suitable, groups can work outside.

3. Tell students to paint all sides of boxes — some plain, others designed.

4. Allow 24 hours for the boxes to dry. Then instruct students to stack them in an interesting way and glue together. (For a very finished look, box towers can be sprayed with shellac.) You may want students to name their tower.

Evaluation:

How well students have manipulated 2- and 3-dimensional shape to express themselves.

Shape/Form Quadrant IV —If?

7. *Left Mode — Analyzing their own application of the concepts for usefulness, originality, and as a stepping stone for future learning.*

Objective

To evaluate the shape of 5 similar objects in a display.

Activity

Students participate in a discussion to review and synthesize all that they have learned about shape. Following the discussion, five assorted mugs (each one distinctly different in shape) are placed on a high table or counter top for the class to view. As students continue to study the design of each mug, have them respond to each question in the questionnaire below. When the class has an opportunity to discuss and evaluate the shape of each mug, ask students to vote for the mug they would most like to own.

Sample Display Questionnaire:

1. How are these ___ similar in shape/form?

2. How do these ___ differ in shape/form?

3. Which ___ has a shape/form that is the most functional?

4. Which ___ has a shape/form that is the most aesthetically pleasing to you?

Students now have the background necessary to create their own shape display. Have students work in small groups to plan and organize a display that can be shared with the entire class. The following items work particularly well in shape displays:

cereal bowls	sun glasses
tea kettles	sun hats
pitchers	baskets
drinking glasses	flower vases
salt and pepper shakers	

Evaluation:

How well students have worked with their group to organize a shape display.

8. *Right Mode — Doing it themselves and sharing what they do with others*

Objective:

To share student Shape Displays.

On the appointed day, each group sets up their shape display in a location where it can be easily viewed by everyone. When it is time for a particular group to share, a group spokesperson holds up each item and discusses its individual shape. Then the class is asked to respond to all four questions on the Shape Display Questionnaire. Finally, a class vote is taken to determine which item students would like to own. The winning shape from each display is placed in a highly visible location referred to as "The Winner's Circle." This culminating display will enable students to become better acquainted with the winning shapes during the remainder of the day or week.

Evaluation:

The quality of each group's shape collection. Did the items in each display lend themselves to a shape/form comparison? How well each group's spokesperson shared individual display items and managed student responses to the shape display questionnaire. Did students have enough information to feel comfortable voting for the item they would most like to own in each display?

Texture

Texture is surface quality revealed through our sense of touch. Everything that we touch has a surface quality. Tactile experience is particularly important to babies and young children. After much direct contact with their environment, they learn that some of the sensation experienced when touching an object can be felt by looking alone. For example, we recognize a smooth sensation when looking at a polished stone even though we have not touched it.

A few people have a natural inclination to perceive the environment primarily by their sense of touch. Psychologists refer to these individuals as "haptics." The haptic individual has adequate vision but prefers touching to vision. Most of us are conditioned to have the opposite tendency. Perhaps we remember our parents' warning not to touch when browsing through a gift shop or when visiting someone else's home. Early in life, many of us learned that it is simply not good manners to touch. So now we often refrain from experiencing new textures or reacquainting ourselves with familiar ones. In time, our understanding of texture may be almost entirely based upon what we see. In separating ourselves from actual texture, our ability to know and enjoy the world is diminished.

The visual sense, partly because we use it so much, is prone to see the larger picture while neglecting the special details. This situation is comparable to visiting a fine restaurant and gulping down an artfully prepared gourmet dinner. By eating large bites, we fail to notice and enjoy the nuances of flavor and texture. If we are to see more of the diverse detail so abundant in our world, it is necessary to rely on help from the nonvisual senses. Since our sense of touch is less capable of perceiving the large picture, it can direct our perception toward the discrimination of particular features. For example, the feathery lines etched on the soft leathery surface of a maple leaf may not be seen unless we explore it with our fingers. As Robert McKim states in *Experiences in Visual Thinking*, "Nature doesn't separate seeing from the other senses, only words do." [14] Seeing is polysensory. By combining the visual and tactile senses, we see more of the detail embedded in the larger patterns of our environment.

Many classroom activities in this unit help our students stay in touch with their world. Holding a multi-textured fashion show, making a texture chart, and creating a burlap nature weaving are among the hands-on experiences which will enable students to develop their tactile sense. Learners also need to be introduced to implied texture, as in a drawing, painting, or photograph. Implied texture must be seen to be felt. Many interesting implied textures can be created with line and/or color. Children easily learn how to create the rough quality of a tree's bark with pencil lines. The texture of rippling water in a pond or the soft wispy fluff of cotton candy can be created with just a few brush strokes.

Texture *Texture* *Texture* Texture Texture

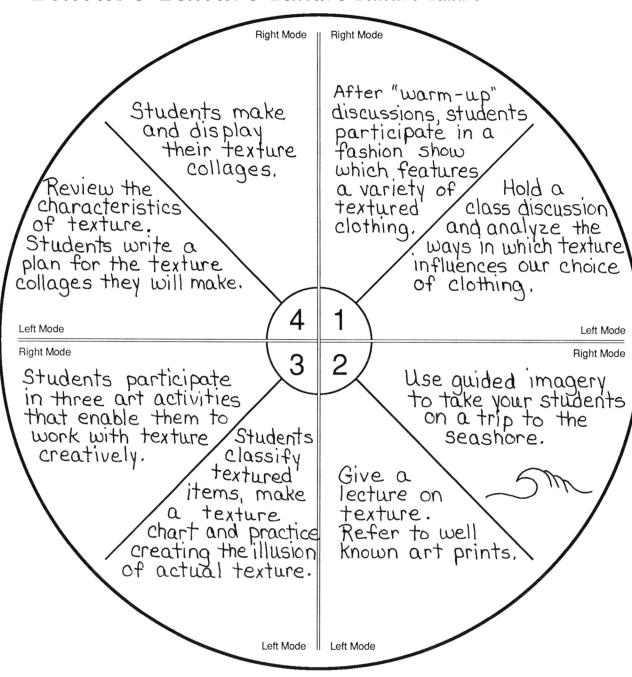

Right Mode | Right Mode

4 1

After "warm-up" discussions, students participate in a fashion show which features a variety of textured clothing.

Hold a class discussion and analyze the ways in which texture influences our choice of clothing.

Students make and display their texture collages.

Review the characteristics of texture. Students write a plan for the texture collages they will make.

Left Mode | Left Mode

Right Mode | Right Mode

3 2

Students participate in three art activities that enable them to work with texture creatively.

Students classify textured items, make a texture chart and practice creating the illusion of actual texture.

Use guided imagery to take your students on a trip to the seashore.

Give a lecture on texture. Refer to well known art prints.

Left Mode | Left Mode

Based on the 4MAT system model by Bernice McCarthy.

Texture Quadrant I — Why?

1. Right Mode — Create the Experience

Objective:

To experience texture by participating in class fashion show.

Activity:

The day you plan the fashion show, discuss textures students are actually wearing. Do a "Blind walk" or an imaginery "fingertip walk" around the classroom. Then make plans to hold a class fashion show which features a rich variety of textured clothing. A silk blouse, wool sweater, denim shirt, leather jacket, velveteen blazer, cotton sweater, and costume jewelry are items that can be used. Invite students to participate as observers and/or models. Plan a short rehearsal the day before so that every model will know where to walk and stand. Choose appropriate background music to enhance this visual-tactile experience.

Evaluation:

The success of the fashion show.
Did students enjoy the many different textures of clothing?

2. Left Mode — Analyze the Experience

Objective:

To discuss the ways in which texture influences our choice of clothing.

Activity:

At the close of the fashion show, ask all models to stand together at the front of the classroom. As students continue to observe the clothing worn by models, pose the following questions for class discussion:

1. Which article of clothing has a texture you would most enjoy wearing? Least enjoy wearing?

2. Does the texture of clothing determine where you will wear it?

3. Does velveteen make you feel different from denim? Explain.

Evaluation:

The quality of student response in the class discussion.

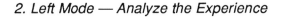

Texture Quadrant II —What?

3. Right Mode — Integrate Reflections into Concepts

Objective:

To acquire a broader appreciation for the aesthetic qualities of texture by taking an imaginary trip to the seashore.

Activity:

Tell your students that their choice of clothing is only one of the ways in which texture can define and enrich their lives. Ask them if they have been to the ocean. Take a few moments to let them share some of their experiences. Then read the guided imagery below to take students on an imaginary trip to the beach.

Close your eyes... Imagine yourself sitting on a warm sandy beach, facing a deep blue ocean... Pick up a handful of sand... Look closely at the multitude of tiny grains... Experience the texture of the sand... Take a pinch of it and rub it between your fingers... Notice how it feels... Now let the grains fall gently through your fingers... Reach deep down into the sand... Notice how it becomes cool and moist... Find a piece of driftwood... Run your fingers across its hard, smooth surface... Inspect each ridge, depression, and finely etched line... Overhead you hear the sounds of sea gulls screeching... You see one of their feathers drifting downward... Reach for the feather. Now it is yours. See every line and edge of it... The tip... And the fluff around the quill... Pick up the feather and brush it across the back of your hand... Your cheek... Think about how it feels.

Keeping your eyes closed, look to your right and left. Notice how far the beach extends on either side of you... Feel the warmth of the sun... Feel the gentle ocean breeze whisper in your ear... Brush the sand off yourself and take a walk along the beach barefoot. Your feet sink into the wet sand with each step... Feel the waves washing against the shore... Notice the rhythm of the tide as it moves in and out...in and out...each time washing over your feet and then pulling the sand out from under them. A piece of seaweed catches on one of your toes as the tide is moving out. Feel its slippery mass as you reach down to remove it... Throw it up into the air and see how it glistens in the sunlight before it falls back into the water. Very slowly inhale the salty air.. Exhale... Inhale... Take one last look at the ocean...the sky...the gulls... and the long stretch of sandy beach... Remember all of the textures you have enjoyed during your trip to the ocean. Now very slowly open your eyes.

Following the imagery, allow student to share their most vivid images. Ask them to think of one texture they especially enjoyed during their trip to the ocean.

Evaluation:

How much students enjoyed their trip.

4. Left Mode — Develop Theories and Concepts

Objective:

To provide a formal definition of texture.
To become knowledgeable about the characteristics of texture.
To become acquainted with the expressive use of texture.

Activity:

Give a lecture on texture. Before the lecture, display a collection of art prints that exhibit various characteristics of texture. The following artists emphasize and use texture creatively in their work: Jackson Pollock, Juan Gris, Constantin Brancusi, Vincent Van Gogh, and Arthur Dove. Include some of all of these concepts in your lesson.

1. Definition of Texture
   Texture is the actual or visual feel of a surface. It may be produced by natural forces or by manipulations of the materials.

2. Kinds of Texture
   Natural: Textures that occur naturally on surfaces in the environment. *Manmade:* Textures that occur on the surfaces of manmade materials.

3. Characteristics of Texture
   a. The surface quality can feel rough or smooth.
   b. The surface quality of a texture can vary from coarse to fine.
   c. When subjected to pressure, the texture can feel hard or soft.
   d. The touch will detect moisture qualities and the texture will feel wet or dry.
   e. The touch will detect a temperature range from warm to cool.
   f. Visual qualities of a texture are affected by how the surface reflects light...from shiny to dull.

4. Texture is used to stimulate tactile responses in the following ways:
   Actual texture — Surface qualities of a real object or material.
   Visual texture — Illusion or feeling of texture to the eye.
   Simulated texture — Imitations of real texture (false brick).
   Invented texture — Patterns which are made-up elements repeated in a rhythmic or random manner.

5. Design Principles
   Texture can be used to show contrast, directional movement, repetition, balance, positive/negative space, and dominance.

6. Expressive Use of Texture
    Texture can be used to express or enhance an emotional feeling in a composition. Fluffy, soft textures create feelings of warmth and are inviting. Hard, slick surfaces seem cool and impersonal.

Evaluation:

Objective quiz.

Texture Quadrant III — How?

5. Left Mode — Working on Defined Concepts

Objective:

To use their knowledge of the characteristics of texture to classify a variety of objects.

To make a texture chart and practice drawing lines and patterns which can be interpreted as visual texture.

Activities:

#1 —Collecting and Classifying

Divide the class into 5 groups. Assign one of the following texture categories to each group:

Rough <—> Smooth   Hard <—> Soft

Coarse <—> Fine   Wet <—> Dry

Shiny <—> Dull

Ask each group to collect and bring to class 7-10 textured items that fall within their assigned category. When all collections have been brought to class, direct the groups to lay out their items and place them on a continuum from hard to soft, shiny to dull, etc. This may be a difficult task at times because some items are so similar in texture. Students will need to concentrate on the actual rather than the visual texture when they are faced with a difficult decision. Be sure that each group makes a written record of the continuum. Then provide enough time for all groups to visit and classify all 5 of the texture collections. When this has been accomplished, discuss the results. Ask students if any of the items belonging to a particular category could also be placed and categorized in another category. For example, a piece of sandpaper could be placed in the rough - smooth category but it could also be added to the coarse - fine collection.

ACTUAL TEXTURE	VISUAL TEXTURE	DESCRIPTIVE WORDS	DAILY USES	CREATIVE USES
BURLAP				
FOIL				
COTTON				

Illustration A

#2 - Making a Texture Chart

What You Need:

A class set of texture chart outlines (See illustration A.)
A 1" square piece of burlap and foil for each student
Cotton balls
Glue

What To Do:

1. Provide each student with a texture chart outline, a 1" piece of burlap and foil, a cotton ball, and glue.

2. Tell students to glue the burlap, foil, and cotton ball in column one of the texture chart.

3. Ask students to draw a visual representation of each texture in the 2nd column.

4. In column three have students write down words which describe each of the three textures.

5. Columns five and six provide an opportunity for students to think about the possible uses for burlap, foil and cotton. Encourage students to be resourceful and inventive as they fill in these spaces.

6. When all charts have been completed, discuss the similarities and differences of the recorded responses. Encourage students to add additional data to their chart during the discussion.

#3 - Creating the Illusion of Texture

Make class sets of work sheets that display the overall shapes of animals, plant life, baskets, food, etc. Ask students to use pencils, markers, or crayons to create lines and patterns which give the illusion of actual texture. Display complete work sheets so that students can see alternative ways to create particular textures.

Evaluation:

The successful completion of all three activities.

---

6. Right Mode — "Messing Around"

Objective:

To explore texture creatively by creating a Kitchen Cupboard Mosaic, a Glossy Tissue Paper Picture, and a Woven Nature Collection.

Activities:

#1 — Kitchen Cupboard Mosaics

What You Need:

9x12 sheets of railroad board or cardboard
Assorted beans, pasta, rice, dried cereal, eggshells, cornmeal, watermelon seeds, coffee beans, popcorn, aluminum foil, and brown paper bags
Paper plates
Glue

What To Do:

1. Ask students to help you bring in some of the items listed above for number two. Be sure that a wide variety of textures and colors are collected.

2. Display the collection and discuss artistic ways to use each of the items. For example, spaghetti could become long straight hair while Grape-Nuts cereal is a natural for creating tree trunks.

3. Write the word mosaic and the following definition on the chalk board.

   Mosaic: A picture composed of many small separate bits of clay, marble, paper, etc., which are to be cemented to a background.

   If possible, show students one or more examples of a mosaic.

4. Provide each student with a sheet of railroad board and a small paper plate. Ask them to sketch on the railroad board an animal, a landscape, a cityscape, a person's face, a still life, or a design. Then invite them to bring their paper plate to the display table so they can collect the items needed to make the mosaics.

---

5. Students complete their mosaics by gluing beans, seeds, etc., onto their railroad board.

6. When glue is dry, mosaics may be sprayed with shellac for a bright, glossy finish.

#2 —Glossy Tissue Paper Pictures

What You Need:

9x12 or 12x18 white drawing paper
Assorted colors of tissue paper
Scissors
White glue
A large bottle of polymer medium
Newspapers
4-5 wide brushes

♪ Let the sun shine in ♪

What To Do:

1. On a table or counter top, arrange several colors of tissue paper so that they are easily accessible to students. Cover the surface of another table with newspaper. Place the bottle of polymer medium and brushes on the newspaper for later use.

2. Provide each student with white drawing paper, scissors, and glue.

3. Hold up a sheet of tissue paper and ask students to describe the texture. Tell students they are going to make pictures with tissue paper. Demonstrate how tissue paper can be cut, overlapped, and glued down on white paper. It can also be crinkled, twisted, and folded.

4. Show students a tissue paper picture that has been brushed with a coat of clear polymer medium. Ask them to describe how the polymer medium changes the visual and actual texture of the tissue paper.

5. Allow one group of students at a time to select the tissue paper they will use.

6. When students have finished gluing pieces of tissue paper onto the white paper, have them brush one coat of polymer medium over their entire picture.

7. Be sure to hang these pictures in a location where sunlight can illuminate their bright, shiny beauty.

Note: Polymer medium is water soluble and can be found in craft and hobby stores. Brushes clean easily if the polymer medium is not allowed to dry on them.

#3 —A Woven Nature Collection

What You Need:

A piece of 7x14 burlap
9" wooden dowels or heavy sticks
Thumb tacks
A collection of leaves, pods, grasses and twigs

What To Do:

1. Have students bring in textures found in nature. (See #4 above.)

2. Give students a piece of burlap. Show them how to pull out a series of threads so that leaves, grasses, or twigs can be woven into the burlap. The pods must be glued.

3. Attach a wooden dowel or heavy stick to each burlap weaving with three thumbtacks. Tie a piece of burlap thread or string to each end of the dowel and hang.

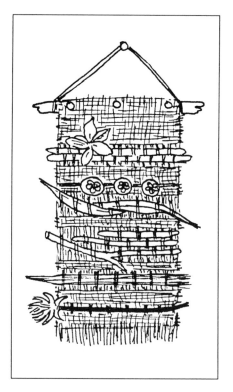

Evaluation:

How well students have worked with a variety of textures to express themselves creatively.

Texture Quadrant IV —If?

7. *Left Mode — Analyzing their own application of the concepts for usefulness, originality, and as a stepping stone for future learning*

Objective:

To review the characteristics of texture.

To make plans to complete a texture collection.

Activity:

Have students list as many of the six categories of texture as they can remember in one minute. Ask everyone to work with a partner. When the time is up, list all six categories on the overhead or chalkboard. Spend some time observing the various attributes of texture present in the students' art work from Quadrant III. Then have students write a paragraph or statement which compares/contrasts actual and visual texture. Discuss their ideas and ask them to think out loud about why actual and visual texture both contribute so much to our enjoyment of the world.

As a culminating experience, students will make a texture collage. A texture collage is an arrangement of various textures pasted or fastened to a flat surface. The textures may be actual (a piece of cloth, wallpaper, dried leaves, pebbles) or visual (magazine pictures, brochures, photographs, wrapping paper), or a combination of both.

Suggested subjects for Texture Collages:

-Hiking in the Mountains
-A Season of the Year
-A Day at the Seashore
-A Party for Friends
-Shopping in the Produce
   Section of the Supermarket
-A Picnic at the Park
-My Ideal Bedroom

Show students how to glue each texture so that it overlaps and fits together. Ask students to write down the subject of their collage and the materials they will use. Check their plan to see if it is realistic and workable.

Evaluation:

Quality of the discussion and student plans for the texture collages.

8. Right Mode — Doing it themselves and sharing what they do with others

Objective:

To make and display a collage for everyone to enjoy.

Activity:

Students make their texture collages. Invite each student to talk about their collage and what they learned about texture while doing it. Display completed collages.

Evaluation:

Did student collages exhibit the following:

-An appropriate theme?
-A variety of textures?
-Satisfactory workmanship?
-An effective design?

wheels of discovery

S o much education uses an "outside-in" approach to learning where students are given the facts and are required to memorize, organize and return them in measurable tests. The visual arts provide a much needed balance to this way of instruction. Jean Mormon Unsworth states, "They offer a way for teachers to tap the potential inside each student and activate the powers that led their earliest ancestors to question, search, experiment, imagine, make connections, and delight in learning."[15] In doing so, they make possible an "inside-out" approach to learning that integrates all the educational experiences of students.

Students who participate in visual arts activities on a regular basis develop another kind of structure for responding to and symbolizing their experiences. They possess the ability to speak to that part of themselves and others that is not dependent on the coding and decoding of verbal language. This ability is especially important in a society where more information is transmitted visually than verbally.

Many teachers are unable to honor this type of student-centered learning. Perhaps they did not have these opportunities in school. Little if any training has been offered that would enable them to feel comfortable providing these experiences for their students. In recent years education has placed increasing emphasis on teaching the "basics" and raising test scores. This focus on rational learning ignores the need for developing creative thought processes. However, an explosion of knowledge regarding brain function has occurred. This awareness has led to new directions for curriculum planning as educators recognize the need for integrating all thought processes in the educational experience. Many ideas come to mind of the kind of art that teaches academics.

1. *Illustrating the reading text*
    Every week I ask students to illustrate one of their stories in the reading text. They are instructed to draw a 4-part sequence representing the main events in the story. Cartoon-like images appear on the paper, complete with conversational bubbles. At first, students depend on the illustrations in the textbook to assist them in completing the assignment. However, in a few weeks they begin to realize that each reader should create her/his own visual images while reading the story. As the year progresses, students include more detail in their drawings. The setting, facial expression of the characters, and clues about the weather all begin to surface. I often display all of the drawings so students can see how others have chosen to interpret the story. The following reading skills are developed when students draw what they have read:

    Better comprehension of main points as well as the essential details. (Students often reread passages before they begin to draw.)

    The order of events in the story.

    The particulars of the setting in which the story takes place.

    Weekly reading quizzes are higher when students have completed this activity. Sometimes I vary this activity by asking them to draw a mini-mural or a character's portrait.

2. *Learning the parts of a flower*
    Every year a third grade teacher I know teaches a unit on flowers. One objective is for students to learn the names and location of each flower part. In the past this skill was taught by having students label each part on a ditto. This approach worked well for some third graders. However, there were many students who simply copied down the names without actually learning them. One year the teachers asked students to create their own flower (real or imaginary) by cutting out construction paper parts. Of course each part had to be labeled. When a quiz was given the next day everyone in the class did well.

3. *Bottle people characterizations*
    When I ask my 5th graders to write a character description about someone they know well, the results are almost always disappointing. Although I teach a lesson and hold a class discussion on how to write this type of a description, students generally write very little. What they do write is dry and lacking in texture and color. One spring I decided to have them create the person they would describe. Everyone brought a soft drink bottle to class. We taped newspaper heads on top and then paper machéd the entire bottle. A few days later each person was given a head of yarn hair, painted fea

tures, respectable clothing, and of course a name. The character descriptions students wrote that year were remarkably rich in detail. I was amazed to learn how many endearing qualities these bottle people had. Once these powerful descriptions had been written, later descriptions about other kinds of people were extremely well-written. (Please refer to the examples of bottle people descriptions on the following page.)

4. *Pictorial timeline*
The sequence of events is important when studying a period in history or reading a story or novel. Students are often confused about the order in which events take place. This confusion can interfere with their ability to build concepts and answer questions about the material. Reading the assigned material again does help some students but not everyone. Years ago I decided to have students create simple pictorial timelines wherever time and order events are particularly important. The results are well worth the time students spend creating visual images. Occasionally students will work together to create a class pictorial timeline depicting the Civil War or early exploration. Time order questions on worksheets and in class discussions show that the visuals students create help them do a better job of remembering.

5. *Salt and flour maps*
Students can read about the location of the Sierra Nevada Mountains or the Great Lakes but they know and remember the location of these landforms when they make a salt and flour map. The Mississippi River becomes more than a name in the history book as they paint thin blue lines on their map. They acquire an overall sense of the physical contour of a particular region. This enables them to understand more about the climate, vegetation and life lived in a particular area.

Before this activity students did not have a clear concept of geography. Most students have only a vague idea about where major landforms are located. Afterwards students could easily define geography in their own words. They had no difficulty locating mountains, valleys, and rivers on a blank map during a test. Months later they could still locate the places they created on their salt and flour maps.

6. *Creating picture storybooks for younger children*
Four or five times a year I have students put the basal readers away for two weeks while we read and study a novel. One year when we had finished reading *Island of The Blue Dolphins*, I decided to have students create their own storybook version of the novel rather than fill in answers to worksheet questions. We would then visit a second grade classroom, assign one fifth grader to share with one second grader, and read the storybooks in pairs. My fifth graders were excited about the plan and they worked hard. It was difficult for them to decide which events should be included. At times they struggled to draw illustrations that would convey the message of the novel. A tremendous amount of learning occurred. Everyone became skilled in summarizing a large body of information both visually and verbally. Students did unusually well on the final test. Some of the second graders were able to convince my fifth graders to gift them with a storybook. However, most students could not imagine parting with a project to which they had given so much of themselves.

Bottle People Character Descriptions

Before the bottle people were created, students wrote brief, uninspired character descriptions. After making the bottle people, the descriptions they wrote were personable, lively, rich in detail. Below are three examples of character descriptions which were later expanded as a result of the bottle people activity.

Before

1. Bart is a boy who has spiked hair. He wears sunglasses, a leather jacket, and Levis 501 jeans. He wears Nike Air shoes like me. Bart is 6 ft. 3 and he can beat up anybody.

2. Jenny had blond hair, blue eyes, and likes to wear bikinis. She drives a Porsche. Jenny is skinny. Her hair is very curly and she has a boyfriend who looks dorky.

3. Cindy is very pretty. Her eyes are kinda brown. She is very tall and slim. A lot of boys like her because she is beautiful. Cindy drives a Ferrari and has lots of clothes.

After

1. Bart is 6 ft. 3 and weighs 302 pounds. He is all muscle, not an ounce of lard. Bart was the World Wrestling Federation champion at one time. He has black, spiked hair and everybody likes him. But don't get him angry. He can be mean.

   Bart is 41 years old. Even though he is older now, his dream is to become the WWF champion once again. He owns a large house in Venice, Calif. and a red convertible Corvette. When Bart is not sunning himself at the beach, he practices different wrestling moves. His favorite moves are the Clothesline, the Boot to the Face, and the Big Leg Drop.

2. Jenny has silky blond hair which is very wavy. She has dark blue eyes and soft pink skin with rosy cheeks. Jenny is shy but friendly. She lives in the country and loves nature. Jenny loves to take walks in the forest. She has made friends with many of the forest animals. When an animal is hurt, she tries to help. To earn money, Jenny collects various seeds and herbs to make relaxing drinks. Jenny's country house is three stories high. The forest animals often wander up to the front porch when they are lonely for Jenny.

3. Cindy is 11 years old. Her hair is golden brown and her eyes are soft brown. Cindy is very tall and slim. At school she likes to let the boys chase her. At home she talks to different boys on the phone for an hour or more. Cindy's mother wants her to be popular but she doesn't like Cindy to talk on the phone every night. When Cindy is not talking on the phone or visiting her friends, she practices the flute or snacks on chocolate chip cookies. Cindy hopes to be a fashion model when she is old enough. She has heard that models make lots of money.

The following instructional units, created by teachers who work in the Visalia Unified School District, include one or more art activities. In this section you will find units appropriate for students at every level, primary through high school. The teachers who created these units believe as I do that visual arts activities can and must be integrated into academic areas. As students travel around these wheels, they discover that learning is a visual as well as a verbal venture.

Perhaps you will find one or more of these wheels appropriate for use in your own classroom. However, it is likely that you will want to create your own Discovery Wheels. I have included a list of visual art activities on this page that can easily be adapted for your instructional purposes. In creating your own wheels, you may wish to refer to Bernice McCarthy's book entitled *The 4MAT System*. As I stated earlier, all of the instructional wheels in *Going Beyond Words* are based on the 4MAT cycle of learning. While each lesson is represented here by a single wheel, some of the more extensive lessons might require a series of interlocking wheels to complete.

Visual Art Ideas

When you are creating instructional units, be sure to include visual art activities. Your students could make a(n)...

- mural
- collage
- scroll theater
- mosaic
- peek box
- watercolor scene
- advertisement
- mask
- yarn picture
- figure bulletin board
- drawing with chalk on wet or dry paper
- block print
- montage
- crayon resist
- banner
- mobile
- book jacket
- diorama
- poster
- comic strip
- pictorial timeline
- clay sculpture
- paper maché
- torn paper design
- paper bag puppet
- bottle people
- burlap stitchery
- stencil pattern

The Dinosaur Kingdom

Right Mode

Quadrant 4 (Right Mode): Students write an imaginary story entitled, "If I had a pet dinosaur..." The stories are illustrated and shared with the class.

Quadrant 4 (Left Mode): Once again ask the class, "What is a dinosaur exactly?" Compare their present ideas with what they said earlier. Reach a consensus about what a dinosaur is and why we should study them.

Quadrant 1 (Right Mode): On the playground use a tape measure or clothesline to show the lengths of zoo animals. Then pace off 70 ft. and ask, "What can this be?"

Quadrant 1 (Left Mode): Discuss what students already know about dinosaurs. Then ask the class, "What is a dinosaur exactly?" Record their responses for later use.

Quadrant 3 (Right Mode): Everyone makes a modeling clay dinosaur. All dinosaurs are placed in a scene complete with rocks, trees and H_2O.

Quadrant 3 (Left Mode): Students complete a fill-in worksheet and draw a picture for each dinosaur. Dinosaur flashcard games help students remember important facts.

Quadrant 2 (Right Mode): Use guided imagery to take students on a journey to the Mesozoic Era. Have them visualize dinosaurs and the environment in which they lived.

Quadrant 2 (Left Mode): Introduce a new dinosaur each day. Teach students about their diet, dimensions and physical characteristics. Also discuss the meaning of their reptile name.

4 1
3 2

Based on the 4MAT system model by Bernice McCarthy.

modeling clay dinosaurs

What You Need:

1. Large pictures of dinosaurs your class has studied

2. 1-2 sticks of modeling clay per student

3. Unlined sheets of 9x12 newsprint paper for sketching

4. Classical music tapes

5. Books and posters which depict dinosaur life

What To Do:

1. Display the dinosaur pictures. Discuss the shapes that make up individual dinosaurs.

2. Pass out pieces of unlined newsprint. Ask students to draw the dinosaur they want to model from clay.

3. Distribute sticks of modeling clay. Encourage students to concentrate and work slowly. Soft background music will help provide a calm, relaxed environment for this activity.

4. Create a Mesozoic Era scene for all of the dinosaurs. Study scenes from books and posters so that you will be able to make it as life-like as possible.

What is Wind?

Right Mode
Right Mode

4 Students write an original poem or story about what it is like to be a kite flying high in the sky. They also make the kite they wrote about. See directions on opposite page.

Discuss students observations about flying a kite. Then review all of the information which has been presented about wind. Students re-read the definition of wind they wrote to see if it needs revision.

1 Read Gilberto and the Wind by Marie Hall Et. Take the class on a walk to find evidence that wind exists. Students record findings in wind journals.

Hold a class discussion about the evidence collected. Use the findings to create a class definition of wind.

Left Mode
Left Mode

Right Mode
Right Mode

3 Take the class outside to fly one or more commercially made kites. Notice how the kites respond to the wind. Have everyone record observations in wind journals.

Students write a sentence for each new wind word in their journal. They draw a diagram which illustrates what causes wind.

2 Distribute sheets of 12"x 18" pieces of white drawing paper. Students draw a picture on one side to show a "windy day". On the other side, they draw a "still day".

Present a lesson on wind. What causes it? What is a tornado? a hurricane?

Left Mode
Left Mode

Based on the 4Mat system model by Bernice McCarthy.

BEYOND WORDS

make your own kite

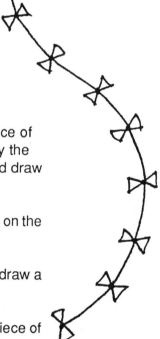

What You Need:

1. Several kite patterns made from tagboard for children to trace

2. A variety of 9x11 colored construction paper

3. Crepe paper

4. Yarn

5. Scissors

6. Stapler

7. Crayons and/or markers

What To Do:

1. Students choose a pattern and a piece of colored construction paper. They lay the pattern on the construction paper and draw around it.

2. The kite shape which has been drawn on the construction paper is cut out.

3. Crayons and/or markers are used to draw a face on the kite.

4. Each student staples an 18-24 inch piece of yarn to the bottom of the kite face.

5. Cut pieces of crepe paper are twisted around the yarn to make bows.

6. Display each kite alongside the story or poem that has been written about it.

The Letter "R" *recognizing the shape and sound*

Right Mode

Each student creates a rock person. Every rock person is given a name that begins with "R". Interesting data about each rock person is recorded and shared.

Right Mode

Sing "Row, Row, Row Your Boat" or another song which emphasizes the sound of the letter "R" at the beginning of a word.

Discuss the importance of the letter "R". Do you hear this sound often? Is it important to know this letter when you are learning to read.

Left Mode

Make a chart listing all the "R" words generated by the collage. Have students create sentences using some of the words.

Left Mode

4 **1**

3 **2**

Right Mode

Students use colored chalk or fingerpaint to practice writing the letter "R". Also they create a class collage made of pictures which identify words beginning with "R".

Read a story containing words which begin with sounds of "R". Students raise their hands whenever they hear a word that begins with this sound. Also use worksheet and workbook activities.

Right Mode

Have each student pantomine a person, thing or object that begins with the "R" sound. Classmates guess which word is being pantomined.

Show the students a card with the letter "R" on it. Model the sound of "R". Students identify and say the sound.

Left Mode

Left Mode

Based on the 4Mat system model by Bernice McCarthy.

rock people

What You Need:

1. A variety of rocks and pebbles of different sizes and shapes

2. Fast-drying glue

3. Tempera, acrylic paints, or magic markers

4. Yarn, pipe cleaners, small beads, etc.

5. Spray shellac

6. A class set of About Me... profiles

What To Do:

1. Ask students to bring in a variety of rocks and pebbles to class that can be used to make rock people.

2. Wash and dry the rocks at least one day before making the people.

3. When it is time for students to build their rock person, show them how to select rocks and pebbles that will look good together. Use the larger rocks for the bodies and the smaller rocks for hands and feet.

About Me ...

1. Name: _Rufus Rock_

2. Age: _7_

3. Interest: _listening to rock music_

4. Favorite Cartoon: _The Flintstones_

4. Demonstrate how to fasten the pieces together using a fast-drying glue.

5. Students use paint or markers to make the features on their rock person.

6. Yarn can be used for hair. Pipe cleaners, beads, and other items can also be used to detail and dress the rock people.

7. Rock people can be sprayed or painted with shellac but this should be done *before* yarn or pipe cleaners are added.

8. Prepare a class set of About Me ... profiles and have each student complete them.

Pioneer Life on the Oregon Trail

Right Mode

Right Mode

Westward Ho!
Each group member builds a conestoga wagon. Individual wagons are then joined together in a wagon train. Presentations are given to share each group's wagontrain, journal and map.

Review and synthesize what students have learned about pioneer life. List and evaluate the personal qualities necessary to be a successful pioneer. Consider who the pioneers of today are.

Left Mode

Divide the class into groups. Each group imagines they are going west in a covered wagon. Have them list what they will need to survive. Compare the lists created by each group. Are some essential items missing from any of the list? Discuss whether it is easier to survive today than it was during pioneer times.

Left Mode

4 1

3 2

Right Mode

Right Mode

The members of each group create an imaginary journal detailing their many adventures & hardships on the trail. Each entry must be dated. Illustrations are encouraged.

Students continue to work with their group throughout this unit. Give each group a large sheet of butcher paper to make a map of the Oregon Trail. This map will guide them on their journey west.

Left Mode

Present a lecture on crossing the Oregon Trail. Assign reading from the text. Use appropriate films and filmstrips.

Students create visual analogies for PIONEER —
A pioneer is ...
A pioneer is like ...

Left Mode

Based on the 4Mat system model by Bernice McCarthy.

building a conestoga wagon

What You Need:

1. A small milk carton for each student (Shoe boxes can also be used.)

2. Brown tempera paint (Mix a small amount of liquid detergent with it if students use milk cartons.)

3. Circular shapes cut from cardboard

4. Brads

5. White construction paper

6. Modeling clay

7. Pipe cleaners

8. Scissors

What To Do:

1. Students cut off one lengthwise panel of the carton. They paint the outside panels of their carton with brown paint.

2. Wheels are added by fastening circular cardboard shapes with brads to the carton.

3. Glue a rectangular piece of white construction paper to the inside of the wagon, leaving a height of at least three inches and the two ends open.

4. Oxen or horses are made from clay and hitched to the wagon with pipe cleaners.

5. Students may wish to make miniature pioneers and supplies to go with their wagon.

Fairytale Lore

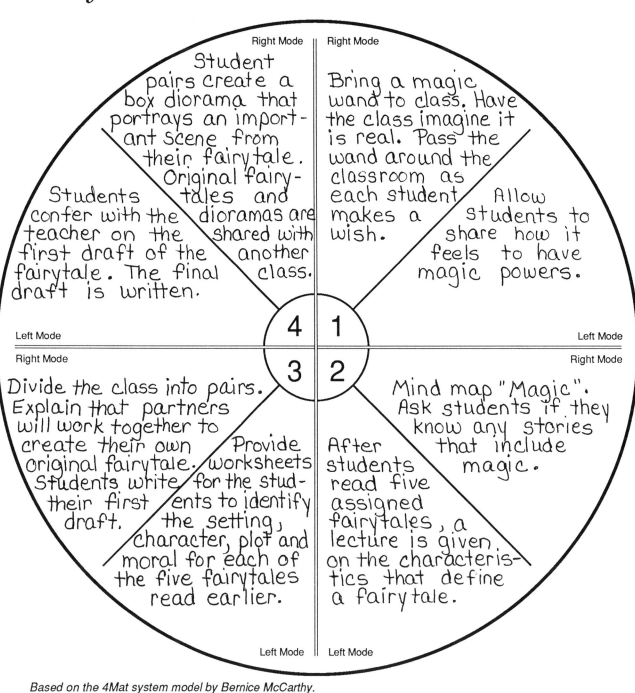

Right Mode (Quadrant 4)
Student pairs create a box diorama that portrays an important scene from their fairytale. Original fairytales and dioramas are shared with another class.

Right Mode (Quadrant 1)
Bring a magic wand to class. Have the class imagine it is real. Pass the wand around the classroom as each student makes a wish.

Left Mode (Quadrant 4)
Students confer with the teacher on the first draft of the fairytale. The final draft is written.

Left Mode (Quadrant 1)
Allow students to share how it feels to have magic powers.

Right Mode (Quadrant 3)
Divide the class into pairs. Explain that partners will work together to create their own original fairytale. Students write their first draft.

Left Mode (Quadrant 3)
Provide worksheets for the students to identify the setting, character, plot and moral for each of the five fairytales read earlier.

Right Mode (Quadrant 2)
Mind map "Magic". Ask students if they know any stories that include magic.

Left Mode (Quadrant 2)
After students read five assigned fairytales, a lecture is given on the characteristics that define a fairytale.

Based on the 4Mat system model by Bernice McCarthy.

fairytale dioramas

What You Need:

1. A sturdy box

2. Scissors

3. Glue

4. Construction paper

5. Tempera paints

What To Do:

1. Ask students to bring a box to class for their diorama. Shoe boxes work well but some projects may need to be housed within larger sized boxes.

2. Use a box to demonstrate the following:

   - The open side becomes the front where the scene is viewed.
   - The top of the box may be open or closed.
   - The background (the inside of the back of the box) can be painted, decorated with cutouts or covered with construction paper or wallpaper.
   - Any decoration should also extend onto the sides.

   Note: Students will enjoy thinking up how to depict their miniature scenes. They will have probably devised many creative ways to represent animals, people, buildings, or plants. Here are a few ideas, though, to get you started:

   Rocks
   Small pebbles
   Chunks of painted sponge

   Fences
   Small twigs
   Toothpicks
   Soda straws
   Spaghetti

   Trees
   Small pine cones
   Green clay
   Painted cotton
   Construction paper cutouts

   Animals and People
   Pipe cleaners
   Clothes pins
   Spools
   Magazine cutouts

Christopher Columbus *Admiral of the Ocean Sea*

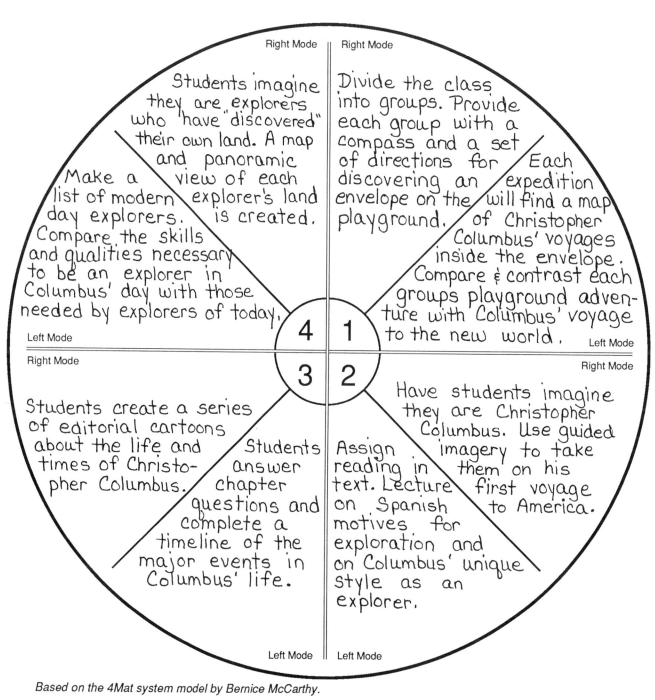

Right Mode — Students imagine they are explorers who "have discovered" their own land. A map and panoramic view of each explorer's land is created.

Right Mode — Divide the class into groups. Provide each group with a compass and a set of directions for discovering an envelope on the playground. Each expedition will find a map of Christopher Columbus' voyages inside the envelope. Compare & contrast each groups playground adventure with Columbus' voyage to the new world.

Left Mode — Make a list of modern day explorers. Compare the skills and qualities necessary to be an explorer in Columbus' day with those needed by explorers of today.

Left Mode — *(section 1)*

Right Mode *(section 4)*

Right Mode — Students create a series of editorial cartoons about the life and times of Christopher Columbus.

Students answer chapter questions and complete a timeline of the major events in Columbus' life.

Right Mode — Have students imagine they are Christopher Columbus. Use guided imagery to take them on his first voyage to America.

Left Mode — Assign reading in text. Lecture on Spanish motives for exploration and on Columbus' unique style as an explorer.

4 1
3 2

Left Mode **Left Mode**

Based on the 4Mat system model by Bernice McCarthy.

a panoramic view of a new land

What You Need:

1. Individual copies of world maps and New Land Profile sheets

2. Large white drawing paper

3. Crayons, markers, and watercolor or tempera paint

4. Bits of fabric, cotton, pebbles, dried leaves, twigs, sandpaper, etc.

What To Do:

1. Distribute individual copies of the world map and the New Land Profile sheet. Students mark the location of their newly discovered land on the map, noting longitude and latitude. New Land Profile sheets are also completed.

2. Discuss the term panoramic view with students. Bring in examples of panoramic photographs to share.

3. Students lightly sketch a panoramic view of their land on scratch paper.

4. The final draft of each student's panoramic view is created on large white drawing paper. Crayons, markers, and paint are used to add color.

Profile of a New Land

1. Location _____

   _____

2. Physical Geography_____

   _____

   _____

3. People_____

   _____

   _____

4. Animal Life _____

   _____

   _____

5. Housing _____

   _____

   _____

5. When the paint is dry, have students use various materials to give each view a 3-dimensional, almost real, quality. Fabric can be used to clothe the people. Dried leaves can be used for vegetation while sandpaper is sometimes used for housing. Students will have many texture ideas once they begin.

The Angles We See: *right, acute, and obtuse*

4 (Right Mode)
Display a collection of abstract art prints. Talk about the lines, angles and shapes within each picture. Students create their own abstract art by making an angle design.

Evaluate the results of the bar graphs. Explore all the reasons why one type of angle is more prevalent than the others.

1 (Right Mode)
For homework, ask students to construct a simple house or structure without using any angles. Students may use whatever material they wish. On the following day, examine the structures which have been made. Discuss any difficulties students encountered. How would our lives be different if there were no angles?

Left Mode | Left Mode

3 (Right Mode)
Students keep an angle journal at home. The number of right, acute and obtuse angles are recorded. In class, students make a bar graph, comparing the no. of right, acute & obtuse angles they found.

Give students a 3"x5" card to practice measuring angles in the classroom. Exercises in the math book are assigned.

2 (Right Mode)
Students experiment with geoboards to better understand the relationship among lines, angles and shapes. Ask them to imagine they are an angle. where would they fit in the classroom?

Provide direct instructions on the three types of angles. Use a large protractor to show students how angles are measured.

Left Mode || Left Mode

Based on the 4Mat system model by Bernice McCarthy.

abstract angle designs

What You Need:

1. A collection of abstract art prints

2. Construction paper strips cut in varying widths and lengths

3. 18x24 white or manila paper

4. Glue and scissors

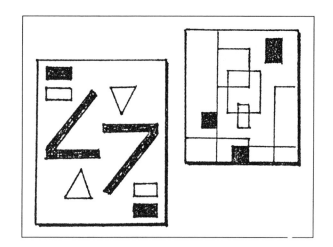

What To Do:

1. Display and discuss a variety of art prints which feature geometric forms. As you talk about the nature of abstract art forms, explain that many artists have found that these forms better convey their attitude and feelings about a subject than by just copying it in a realistic way. Abstract art is a pure example of how the elements of visual language can be used by themselves to express a particular feeling.

2. Distribute sheets of white drawing paper, construction paper strips, glue, and scissors.

3. Students cut and shape paper strips to create an interesting geometric arrangement on the white drawing paper. Be sure they create only designs which are abstract.

4. When students are satisfied with the arrangement they have created, all of the pieces are glued into place.

5. Display the designs alongside the abstract art prints.

6. (Optional) For added fun, ask students to give appropriate titles to some of their designs.

The Renaissance *a time of discovery, invention & art*

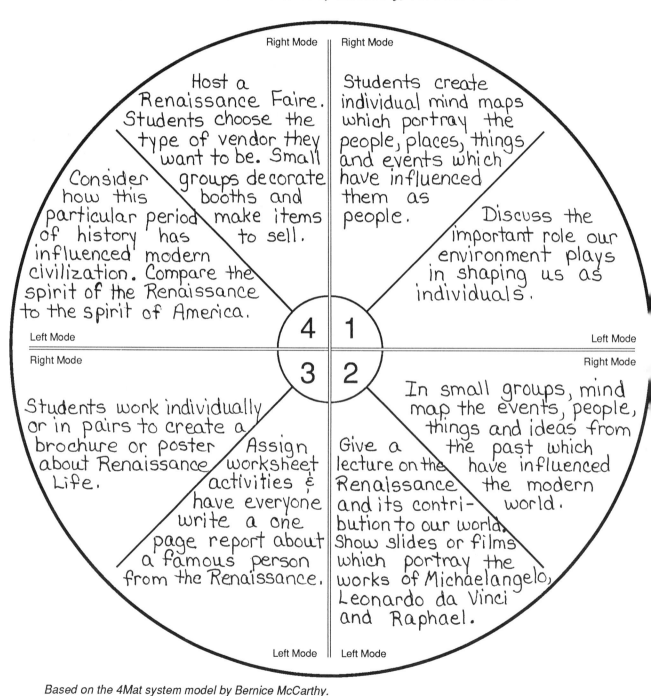

Right Mode

Host a Renaissance Faire. Students choose the type of vendor they want to be. Small groups decorate booths and make items to sell.

Consider how this particular period of history has influenced modern civilization. Compare the spirit of the Renaissance to the spirit of America.

Right Mode

Students create individual mind maps which portray the people, places, things and events which have influenced them as people.

Discuss the important role our environment plays in shaping us as individuals.

Left Mode

4 1
3 2

Right Mode

Students work individually or in pairs to create a brochure or poster about Renaissance Life.

Assign worksheet activities & have everyone write a one page report about a famous person from the Renaissance.

Left Mode

Right Mode

In small groups, mind map the events, people, things and ideas from the past which have influenced the modern world.

Give a lecture on the Renaissance and its contribution to our world. Show slides or films which portray the works of Michaelangelo, Leonardo da Vinci and Raphael.

Left Mode

Left Mode

Based on the 4Mat system model by Bernice McCarthy.

hosting a renaissance faire

1. **Plans and Preparations**

   Mark a date on the calendar and decide where the faire will be held. Students choose what kind of vendors they want to be. Then small groups are formed to plan and decorate a booth. Simple items can be made to sell for a small price. Some examples are given below. Also students can compose simple tunes for food and other goods offered for sale. "Fresh red apples, juicy" or "richly colored cloth, beautiful" call attention to their wares.

2. **Booths**

   a. *Cloth merchants* buy and sell finished cloth of wool, flax, muslin, velvet, and silk. (Sell small squares cut from sheets and tie-dyed.)

   b. *Toy merchants* design dolls, tops, skates, rattles, etc., from wood, clay, cloth, and other common materials. (Sell cardboard dolls.)

   c. *Florists* sell fresh or dried-flower garlands that girls or women wear in their hair.

   d. *Trinket sellers* offer ribbons that people tie around their neck, arms, or belt.

   e. *Weavers* sell any type of woven decoration.

   f. *Herbalists* gather and sell plants whose leaves, roots, and other parts are used to flavor foods or make medicines.

   g. *Candlemakers* make and sell wax candles used for lighting houses.

   h. *Bakers* turn flours of wheat, rye, barley, and other grains into all kinds of bread, rolls, pretzels, etc.

3. **Costumes**

   Boys wear shirts (not tucked in) with puffy sleeves and a rope belt. Fabric strips (used for warmth) are wrapped around pant legs and sandals.

   Girls wear long skirts or dresses. Ribbons are tied around the upper part of blouse sleeves and flowers are worn in the hair.

Writing Camera Eye Descriptions

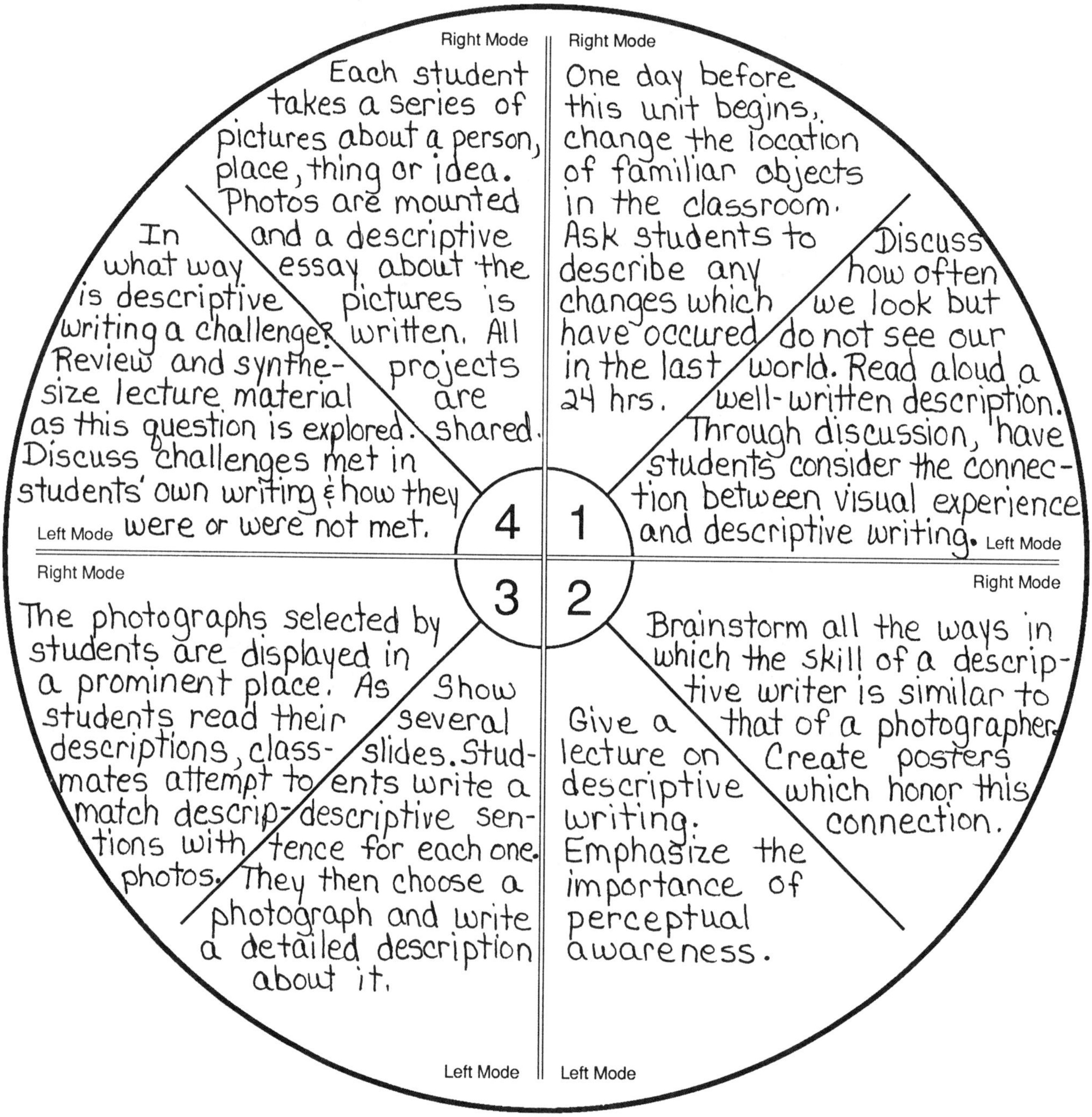

Quadrant 1 (Right Mode):
One day before this unit begins, change the location of familiar objects in the classroom. Ask students to describe any changes which have occured in the last 24 hrs.

Quadrant 1 (continued):
Discuss how often we look but do not see our world. Read aloud a well-written description. Through discussion, have students consider the connection between visual experience and descriptive writing. (Left Mode)

Quadrant 4 (Right Mode):
Each student takes a series of pictures about a person, place, thing or idea. Photos are mounted and a descriptive essay about the pictures is written. All projects are shared.

Quadrant 4 (continued):
In what way is descriptive writing a challenge? Review and synthe- size lecture material as this question is explored. Discuss challenges met in students' own writing & how they were or were not met. (Left Mode)

Quadrant 3 (Right Mode):
The photographs selected by students are displayed in a prominent place. As students read their descriptions, class- mates attempt to match descrip- tions with photos.

Quadrant 3 (continued):
Show several slides. Stud- ents write a descriptive sen- tence for each one. They then choose a photograph and write a detailed description about it.

Quadrant 2 (Left Mode):
Give a lecture on descriptive writing. Emphasize the importance of perceptual awareness.

Quadrant 2 (Right Mode):
Brainstorm all the ways in which the skill of a descrip- tive writer is similar to that of a photographer. Create posters which honor this connection.

Center: 4 1 / 3 2

Based on the 4Mat system model by Bernice McCarthy.

---

photographs that describe

"The camera is an instrument that teaches people how to see without a camera." Dorothea Lange

What You Need:

1. Camera

2. Film
   (black & white or colored)

3. Tagboard
   (18x36 or larger)

Look ...

Frame ...

Focus ...

Shoot ...

What To Do:

1. After explaining the assignment described in quadrant IV on the facing page, provide students with some instruction on using a camera. If you do not have experience in this area, invite a student or guest speaker to give your class some pointers.

   Key concepts to share with students:

   - Photographs can take us to unfamiliar places to see things or cause us to look again and rediscover things we thought we knew well.

   - In photography, time is understood in two ways: 1. for a moment, time and action are stopped; 2. one can find clues in a photograph which place it in an historical time.

   - Framing a photograph means including certain information and excluding or minimizing other information. Relationships are suggested among objects or figures in the frame because they share the same visual space.

2. Discuss appropriate themes or subjects as the basis of a photographic description. A person, an animal, a school-wide event, or a theme such as curiosity are some ideas. Perhaps the most important consideration is for students to photograph things that have personal meaning.

3. After taking a series of pictures, students select their best prints to mount and display on tagboard. They write a descriptive essay and share the entire project.

Portrait of a President

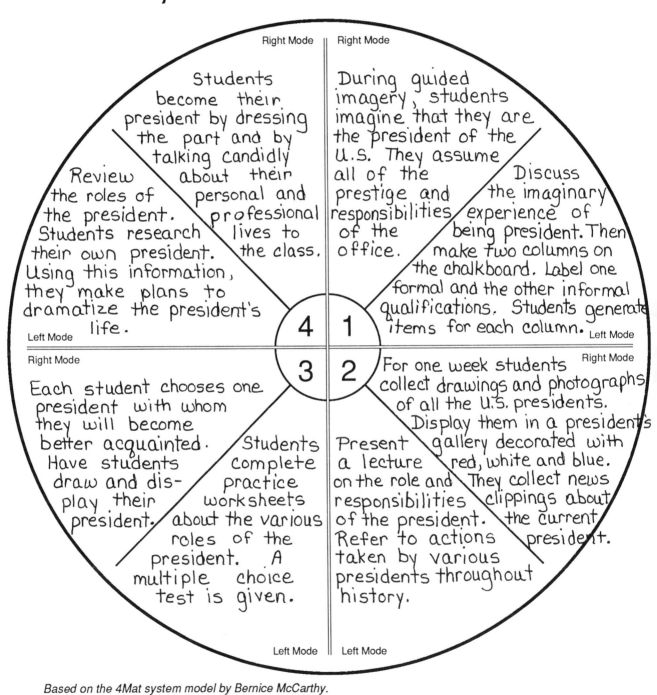

Right Mode

Students become their president by dressing the part and by talking candidly about their personal and professional lives to the class.

Left Mode

Review the roles of the president. Students research their own president. Using this information, they make plans to dramatize the president's life.

Right Mode

During guided imagery, students imagine that they are the president of the U.S. They assume all of the prestige and responsibilities of the office.

Discuss the imaginary experience of being president. Then make two columns on the chalkboard. Label one formal and the other informal qualifications. Students generate items for each column.

Left Mode

4 1

3 2

Right Mode

Each student chooses one president with whom they will become better acquainted. Have students draw and display their president.

Students complete practice worksheets about the various roles of the president. A multiple choice test is given.

Left Mode

Present a lecture on the role and responsibilities of the president. Refer to actions taken by various presidents throughout history.

Right Mode

For one week students collect drawings and photographs of all the U.S. presidents. Display them in a president's gallery decorated with red, white and blue. They collect news clippings about the current president.

Left Mode

Based on the 4Mat system model by Bernice McCarthy.

draw your president

What You Need:

1. 9x12 white drawing paper

2. Photographs or drawings of
   the president each student
   will draw

3. Pencil

4. Crayons or pastels

5. Fine-tipped markers

JAMES GARFIELD

What To Do:

Before students begin drawing,
spend some time discussing a
sequence to use in drawing
faces. Here are some suggested
steps:

1. **Basic shape of the face**

   Draw an outline on the board of different types of facial shapes. For example,
   there are round, square, oval, and heart-shaped faces. Study pictures of the
   various presidents and identify the shape of each face.

2. **Positioning the features on the face**

   Draw an example of figure 1 on the chalkboard.
   Place a midline down the center of the face. Put an
   X about where the hairline starts. Many students
   have a tendency to place the hairline and the eyes
   too high. It is also a good idea to make a light dotted
   line for the eyeline, noseline, and mouthline.

   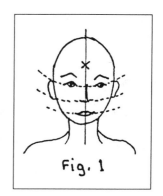

   Fig. 1

3. **Drawing individual features**

   Advise students to practice drawing a president's features on a piece of scratch
   paper before drawing them on the actual portrait. Concentration and attention
   to detail are particularly important during this step.

Beowulf *a test of courage*

Quadrant 4 (Right Mode):
Divide the class into small groups. Each group writes an epic poem about a modern day hero who, like Beowulf, must test his courage. Select background music and share.

Quadrant 4 (Left Mode):
Discuss and analyze Beowulf's growth as a hero. Compare Beowulf to the modern day heroes discussed in quadrant I.

Quadrant 1 (Right Mode):
Divide students into small groups. Ask each group to nominate someone for an honored place in the "Hero Hall of Fame". Record each name in the "Hall of Fame".

Quadrant 1 (Left Mode):
Make a combined list of the qualities their heroes have. Discuss the difference between a hero and a wimp.

4 1

3 2

Quadrant 3 (Right Mode):
Students draw their own personal monster. They also write a detailed description. Drawings are anonymously displayed. Descriptions are read aloud to see if drawings and descriptions can be matched.

Quadrant 3 (Left Mode):
Complete vocabulary exercises and rewrite one section of the poem in modern English. Give a quiz.

Quadrant 2 (Right Mode):
Have student pairs. create a metaphor or simile for hero. Example: A hero is like a diamond.

Quadrant 2 (Left Mode):
Introduce Beowulf by discussing the historical events of this time. Students read and study the poem. Compare and contrast the three battles Beowulf fought.

Based on the 4Mat system model by Bernice McCarthy.

color and paint a monster

What You Need:

1. Colored wax crayons

2. Black poster paint

3. White drawing paper

4. Paintbrushes

What To Do:

1. Paint a shape on a sheet of white paper using black poster paint or black drawing ink.

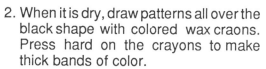

2. When it is dry, draw patterns all over the black shape with colored wax craons. Press hard on the crayons to make thick bands of color.

3. Use the handle of a paintbrush to scratch black patterns and shapes in the colored crayon. (See the monster at the top of the page.)

Cell Design

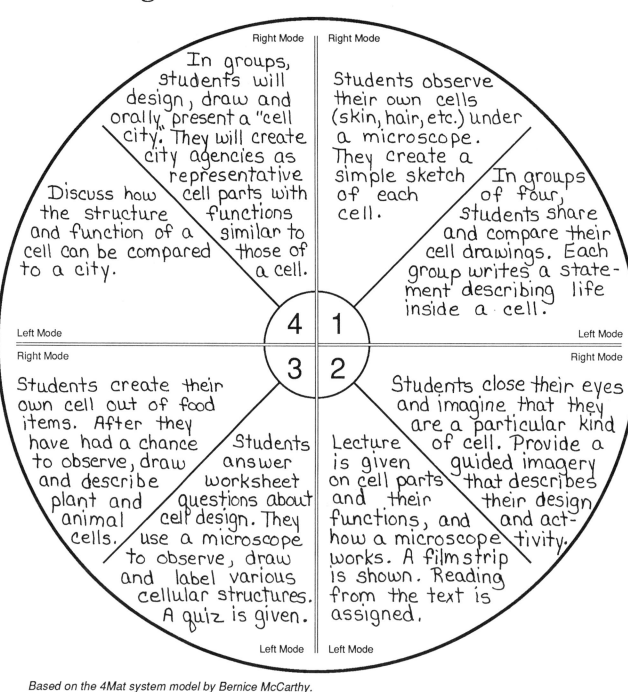

Right Mode (Quadrant 4)
In groups, students will design, draw and orally present a "cell city". They will create city agencies as representative cell parts with functions similar to those of a cell.

Discuss how the structure and function of a cell can be compared to a city.

Left Mode (Quadrant 4)

Right Mode (Quadrant 1)
Students observe their own cells (skin, hair, etc.) under a microscope. They create a simple sketch of each cell.

In groups of four, students share and compare their cell drawings. Each group writes a statement describing life inside a cell.

Left Mode (Quadrant 1)

4 1
3 2

Right Mode (Quadrant 3)
Students create their own cell out of food items. After they have had a chance to observe, draw and describe plant and animal cells.

Students answer worksheet questions about cell design. They use a microscope to observe, draw and label various cellular structures. A quiz is given.

Left Mode (Quadrant 3)

Right Mode (Quadrant 2)
Students close their eyes and imagine that they are a particular kind of cell. Provide a guided imagery that describes their design and activity.

Lecture is given on cell parts and their functions, and how a microscope works. A filmstrip is shown. Reading from the text is assigned.

Left Mode (Quadrant 2)

Based on the 4Mat system model by Bernice McCarthy.

BEYOND WORDS

designing a cell city

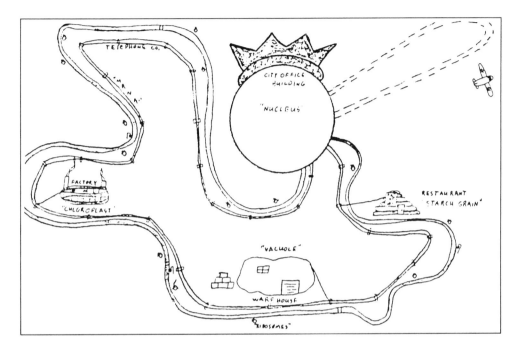

What You Need:

    1. 9x12 unlined newsprint

    2. Large sheets of white drawing paper (12x18 or 18x36)

    3. Pencils

    4. Rulers

    5. Colored markers and/or pencils

What To Do:

    1. Review structure and function of a cell.

    2. List a variety of city agencies on the board or overhead and relate them to the design, function, and processes of a cell.

    3. Divide the class into small groups.

    4. Distribute sheets of unlined newsprint to each group. Ask groups to make their first draft in pencil on the newsprint.

    5. When the first draft is okayed, provide each group with a sheet of white drawing paper and colored markers and/or pencils.

Patterns and Designs *an introduction to geometry*

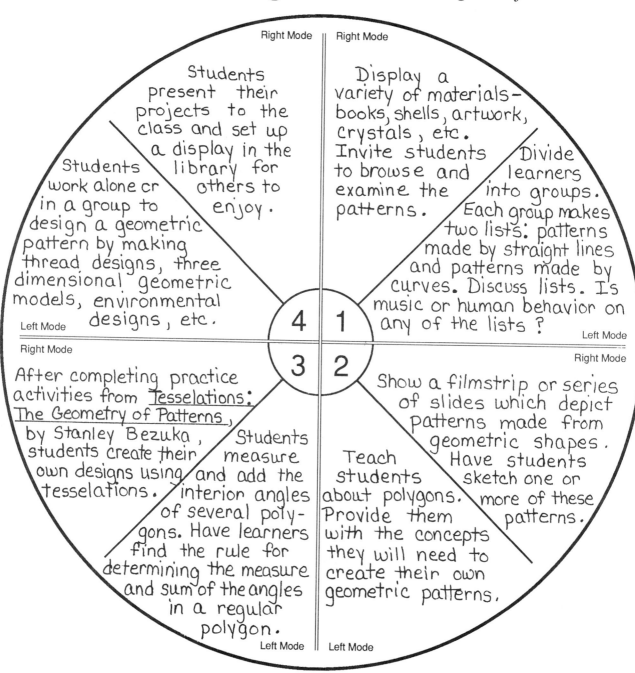

Right Mode — Students present their projects to the class and set up a display in the library for others to enjoy.

Left Mode — Students work alone or in a group to design a geometric pattern by making thread designs, three dimensional geometric models, environmental designs, etc.

4

Right Mode — Display a variety of materials— books, shells, artwork, crystals, etc. Invite students to browse and examine the patterns.

Right Mode — Divide learners into groups. Each group makes two lists: patterns made by straight lines and patterns made by curves. Discuss lists. Is music or human behavior on any of the lists?

1

Right Mode — After completing practice activities from <u>Tesselations: The Geometry of Patterns</u>, by Stanley Bezuka, students create their own designs using tesselations.

Left Mode — Students measure and add the interior angles of several poly- gons. Have learners find the rule for determining the measure and sum of the angles in a regular polygon.

3

Right Mode — Show a filmstrip or series of slides which depict patterns made from geometric shapes. Have students sketch one or more of these patterns.

Left Mode — Teach students about polygons. Provide them with the concepts they will need to create their own geometric patterns.

2

Based on the 4Mat system model by Bernice McCarthy.

thread designs

What You Need:

1. Tag board (9x12 or larger)

2. Tape

3. Thread in various colors

4. Large needles

5. Rulers

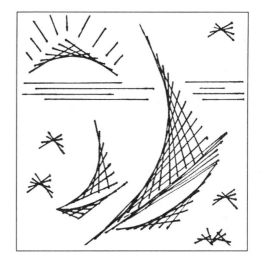

What To Do:

1. With a pencil and ruler draw two lines that form an angle on a piece of cardboard. Draw one line longer than the other. The angle you make can be a right, acute, or obtuse angle.

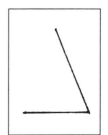

2. Start at the point where the two lines come together. On each line mark the same number of evenly placed dots. The spaces between the dots on the long line will be wider than those you have marked off on the short line.

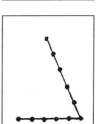

3. Number the dots 1, 2, 3, and so on, as shown. Then make holes through the dot marks with a needle.

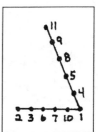

4. Thread your needle and start it under the cardboard. Be sure to tape the thread down in the back. Bring the needle up through hole 1, over and in through hole 2, out at 3, down through 4, out at 5, down through 6, out at 7. Continue doing this until the threading is finished.

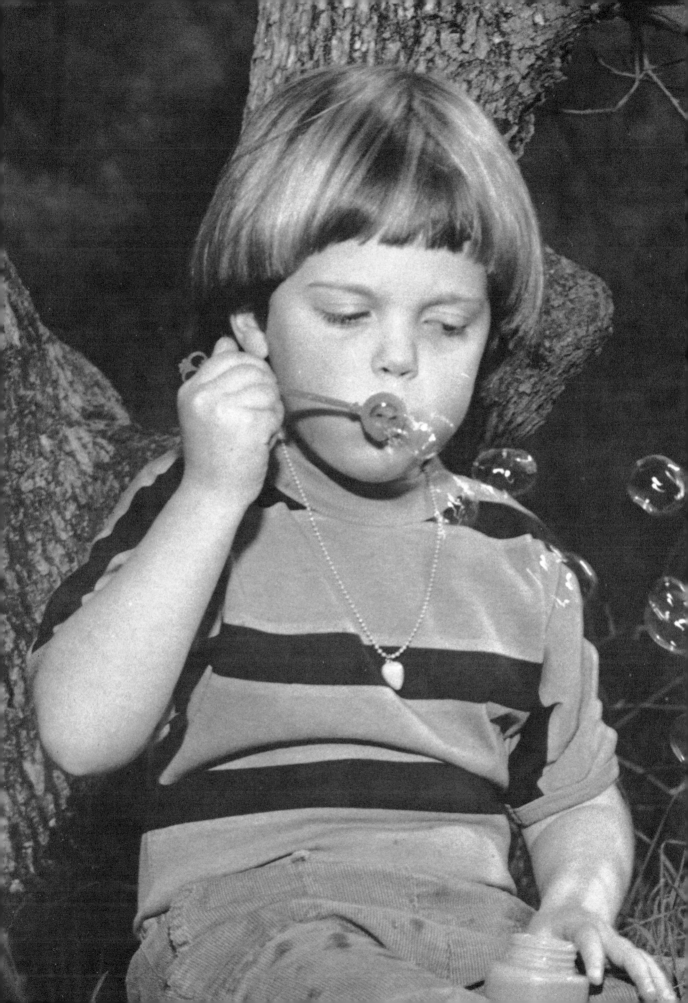

edison and his eggs

When the artist is alive in any person, whatever his kind of work may be, he becomes an inventive, searching, daring, self-expressive creature. He becomes interesting to other people. He disturbs, upsets, enlightens, and he opens ways for a better understanding. Where those who are not artists are trying to close the book, he opens it, shows there are still more pages possible.

Robert Henri
The Art Song

We cannot start early enough in life. There are no limitations. Expose the baby to the lulling noise of a brook. Let him listen to the singing of a bird, the hushing of the wind through the trees, make him aware of the brittle sounds of the fall foliage under your feet. Let him hold and touch whatever the opportunity offers. Open his eyes to whatever you are able to take in. One of my most precious memories is the moment in my childhood when I walked with my mother through the fields and saw the miracles of nature she made me see. Whatever you can do to encourage your child in the sensitive use of his eyes, ears, fingers and entire body will increase his reservoir of experience...

Viktor Lowenfeld

developing perceptual awareness

"We are neglecting the gift of comprehending things by what our senses tell us about them. Concept is split from percept..." Rudolf Arnheim

In learning to cope with our world, we have conceptualized almost everything that we perceive. We place the elements of our experience into general categories, giving names to the categories so that we can think about them and communicate our ideas about them to others. The system created by this process of classification is called a "cognitive system." This system provides a framework for our perception. We could not get along without such classification. However, labeling and categorizing the elements of our world ignores the unique qualities of objects and events and emphasizes those qualities believed to be held in common. It is important to realize that each of us has acquired a particular way of looking at the world that is not the way the world actually is but is simply the way our group conventionally looks at it.

Frequently we limit what comes in through the senses by our immediate dependence on words and concepts. We see "chair," "tree," or "bird," but we do not see this particular chair, tree, or bird. We must learn to use our senses. A state of expanded awareness can be reached only when the mind works in harmony with the senses. To accomplish this, the mind must be open enough to receive what the senses bring in. Duanne Prebble, author of *Art Creates Man Creates Art*, states that "the eyes are blind to what the mind cannot see."[16]

We are all guided in our perceptions by the people we emulate. One of the most important things that a teacher can help students retain as they mature is their sensory awareness of experience. The creative person is open to experience and, in this respect, childlike. Young children absorb much raw data without deciding what to collect or how it will be used. How much information is collected and what is eventually done with it will determine their creative potential not only as children, but as adults.

The Nature of Art and Creative Thinking

"...A first-rate soup is more creative than a second-rate painting. "
Abraham Maslow

It is possible to be a creative person without becoming a professional artist. While true that artists are very creative people, art as a creative process traverses all fields. There are creative bricklayers, doctors, electricians, teachers, and salesmen. To fully understand this point, we must realize that not all creative people deal in special talent products. An individual's type of creativeness refers to his or her ideas, feelings, and human experiences. In a general sense, creativeness can be thought of as a special way of perceiving, learning, and thinking.

What do the experts say about creativity? The following authorities represent the sciences and visual arts. Here is what they have to say about creativity:

Creativity is a process of individual experience which enhances the self. It is an expression of one's uniqueness. To be creative then is to be oneself.
Michael F. Andrews

Creativity is an instinct which all people possess, an instinct with which we were born. It is the instinct which we primarily use to solve and express life's problems ... Creativity, the ability to explore and investigate, belongs to one of the basic drives, a drive without which man cannot exist.
Viktor Lowenfeld

Creativity as interactive learning brings in life. The process becomes a matter of responsiveness to all in life that is coming in and going out, and thus refers to a continual process of rejecting and accepting, making and destroying, revising and adding, and failing and succeeding.
Robert C. Burkhart

The creative person is both more primitive and more cultured, more destructive and more constructive, crazier and saner, than the average person.
Frank Barron

... Creative thinkers are flexible thinkers. They readily desert old ways of thinking and strike out in new directions ... In the area of creativity one should certainly expect to find a trait of originality.
J. P. Guilford

My subjects were different from the average person in another characteristic that makes creativity more likely. Self-actualizing people are relatively unfrightened by the unknown, the mysterious, the puzzling, and often are positively attracted by it.
Abraham H. Maslow

The creative process requires the ability to freely and consciously manipulate the elements of perceptual experience. This dynamic process involves both awareness and action. It might be said that the creative process involves an encounter between the individual and the world. To create is to put two or more known things together in an unusual way, thus creating something new, an unknown thing. There are as many ways to do this as there are creative people. Some of us have never been asked to be creative. Yet creativity can be developed. We can learn to improve ourselves and our world. We can purposely seek new relationships between ourselves and our environment.

By looking carefully at the combined statements of the experts, we can identify some abilities which are unique to creative people. Creative people seem to have many abilities in common:

1. Creative people are alert perceptually.
   They continually explore the world with all of their senses.
   They have the ability to wonder, to be curious.

---

2. Creative people are open to new experiences and ideas.
   They like to experiment with new approaches and media.
   They can see the familiar from an unfamiliar point of view.
   They seek to extend the boundaries of their thinking.

3. Creative people are builders of their ideas.
   They like to rearrange old ideas into new relationships.
   They have the ability to generalize in order to see the universal application of ideas.

4. Creative people like to visualize or imagine new possibilities.
   They like to imagine or pretend.
   They like to dream about new possibilities.

5. Creative people are confident in themselves.
   They are independent.
   They have the ability to be themselves in the face of opposition.

The picture of the creative person developed thus far is that of one who creates out of a vast store of knowledge. Some of this knowledge is conceptual, but a great deal of it is perceptual. It is evident that the creative person has specific attributes and abilities that are used during the creative process. However, to think of creativity as being limited to only those with "inherited talent" is a mistake. The attributes and abilities characteristic of creativity can be developed by all of us. One wonderful way to do so it through art. Classroom teachers who provide a quality art program enable their students to think and function creatively.

Throughout the year students need opportunities to paint, build, and sculpt. By expressing ideas in a visual language, they become flexible and imaginative in their thinking. Our educational system has generally failed to nurture the development of creative imagination. From kindergarten to graduate school, opportunities to develop sensory awareness and creativity are rare. What is thought to be a complete education often promotes the absorption and retention of information at the expense of creativity. Many teachers ignore opportunities to take advantage of the creative imagination possessed by their students because they are not encouraged to do so and because their own imaginations have been stifled.

Perhaps the direct and very powerful connection which exists between art and creativity will be better understood and appreciated by the educational system in years to come. Students who aspire to work in science industry, medicine, business, or education will need to study the body of knowledge in their field. But they will also need to experiment with ideas and imagine new possibilities. Art education provides a fertile means for nurturing the creative potential so necessary to work successfully in these fields and many others. Participation in art experiences should be viewed as more than one component of the creative process ... it is the creative process.

Awareness and the Creative Process

To better understand how important awareness is, it is worth considering how awareness fits into the creative process. In *Developing Artistic and Perceptual Awareness*, Earl Linderman and Don Herberholz define the four essential attributes of the creative process as follows:

1. Awareness
2. Focus
3. Working Process
4. Art Product[17]

The first stage, awareness, is crucial to creativity of any kind. Awareness involves learning to take in an abundance of information without prejudging or categorizing it. An artist deliberately tries to take in more information than other people so that it can be processed and selectively used during the second stage, focusing. Focusing occurs when we begin to narrow the field of data. The artist searches over the information perceived during the awareness stage in an attempt to relate ideas, facts, sense impressions, and feelings. In doing so, (s)he begins to structure bits of information, to make form out of the formless. During this stage it is important to keep ideas fluid. When the artist begins to shape the data into a design or idea, the data is sometimes found to be incomplete or irrelevant. It then becomes necessary to go back to the awareness stage for additional input. Awareness and focus are closely interrelated. A kind of natural rhythm evolves as the individual strives to create or work out the focus that will serve as the blueprint for producing the art product. Stage three, the working process, refers to the production part of creativity. At this time the technical skills of the artist come into play. Stage four, the art product, occurs when the artist's creation is complete. The finished product is the culmination of all the previous stages.

Another view of the creative process or act of learning comes from Bruner and also emphasizes the importance of perceptual awareness. He divides the act of learning into three phases:

1. Acquisition of Knowledge
2. Transformation
3. Evaluation[18]

Perceptual awareness, the taking in of knowledge, is of primary importance in the creative process. For example, visual knowledge of an apple gives its color, texture, shape, line, and pattern of light. If we attend to the apple from this point of view, the "visual knowledge" and recall will be increased because specific details were taken in at the time of viewing. The transformation phase is comparable to the focus and working process stages given above. It is during this part of the creative process that the individual can decide how to transform the knowledge which has accumulated during the awareness stage. The evaluation phase is vital because without it the inner demands of the individual remain diffuse and unrealized. The artist's motivation to reach deeper levels of knowledge and involvement is likely to diminish.

In the 19th century German physiologist and physicist Herman Helmholtz described his scientific discoveries in terms of three distinct stages. Helmholtz named the first stage saturation, which occurs when a wealth of information is taken in through the different senses. The second stage, incubation, is a period of time when the individual mulls over the information. A period of uneasiness and confusion often ensues. The third stage, illumination, occurs when a moment of insight occurs and a solution seems to present itself. In 1908 Henry Poincaré, a French mathematician, suggested a 4th stage, verification. Poincaré described the stage of verification as a time to put the solution into concrete form while checking it for error and usefulness. His four stages are:

1. Saturation
2. Incubation
3. Illumination
4. Verification[19]

All three models of the creative process are similar in content but differ in the number of stages and/or terminology used. While all of the stages in each model are essential to the creative process, I believe that it is important to educators to pay particular attention to stage one. Awareness, acquisition of knowledge, and saturation are terms which emphasize the importance of attending to and perceiving one's environment in great detail from many points of view. Teaching students to be more aware of their surroundings should be a necessary part of any program. Our students cannot function creatively in a vacuum. They need an ongoing, abundant source of perceptual information which can be used to bring forth a personalized visual statement. Now the question remains, how can we help them become more perceptually aware?

Developing Our Own Perceptual Awareness

An example of how closed adults are to their environment is indicated in the following passage:

Helen Keller tells of a friend of hers who walked through the woods. When she was asked what she saw on her walk, she replied, "Nothing in particular." Miss Keller could not imagine how anyone could possibly walk through the woods and see "nothing in particular." Helen Keller must "see" through her fingers, because she lost her eyesight through severe illness when she was a very small child. Yet Miss Keller can appreciate the symmetry, texture, and variety of leaves. She thrills at the touch of the birch tree and the tough bark on the elm tree. She delights at the feel of the first buds on the branches and the special fragrance that announces it is springtime.[20]

To assist our students in developing awareness, we must be open and sensitive to our own experiences. Awareness requires daily practice. Be alert to what nature is doing. The grace of a high-flying bird, the soft beauty of a newly formed blossom, and the symphony of wind playing in the trees can touch your life in a special way. Watch ordinary things with close attention. Have you ever wondered about the myriad of coarse, intertwining lines that encompass the surface of a cantaloupe? Have you taken time to explore the inside of a bell pepper or observe the cream-colored pattern on top of a crab

three models which
represent the creative process

Model A

1. Awareness

2. Focus

3. Working Process

4. Art Product

Linderman & Herberholz

Model B

1. Acquisition of
    Knowledge

2. Transformation

3. Evaluation

Bruner

Model C

1. Saturation

2. Incubation

3. Illumination

4. Verification

Helmholtz & Poincaré

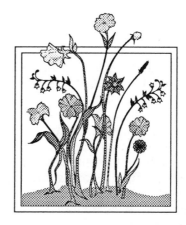

shell? The key to richer awareness lies in the development of our sensory equipment. We must learn to inquire, search, examine, tinker, and experiment. Nothing in our environment is too small or unimportant to overlook. As Lowenfeld states, "Unless we penetrate into an experience, whatever its nature may be will remain superficial and as such cannot serve as the basis for creativity."[21]

The Three Elements of Perceptual Awareness

There are three elements of perceptual awareness that need to be recognized and incorporated into our daily lives. The first element is experience. How accessible do we make ourselves to new and varied experiences? When we change our address, ride in a hot air balloon, or vacation in another country, the world expands as we add to our collection of perceptual knowledge. However, much simpler experiences are also of value and can be enjoyed far more often. Tasting a new flavor of ice cream or taking an unaccustomed walk at sunrise can add a rich dimension to life.

The second element of perceptual awareness is attention to detail. The details of life often escape our attention simply because many of us have not disciplined ourselves to notice them. Of course it is impossible to attend to all of the details in our environment but anyone can increase the number of specific bits of information they remember by being more observant. To become more skilled as an observer:

1. Be curious!
2. Make optimum use of all 5 senses whenever you explore any part of the environment.
3. Continually ask yourself questions about the details of your experiences.

Think back to a time when you found yourself looking at an unusually beautiful flower. Did you wonder about how hard or soft the petals were, the amount of moisture in the flower, how the color in the petals changes or blends, how it smells, and how the flower might taste? These and many other questions help the observer to see and remember the special details.

The third and final element of perceptual awareness is empathy or identification with a given object. Experiences and details are of vital importance, but it is difficult to fully understand an object unless we can allow ourselves to mentally become that object for a short while. When Thomas Edison was a boy, he was always trying to learn more about the world so he asked his father and the townspeople dozens of questions from early dawn until dark. But sometimes asking questions was not enough. One day Tom saw a mother goose sitting on a nest of eggs. Tom wanted to have a deeper understanding of this ritual so he gathered up a dozen eggs, sat down and tried it too. When we allow ourselves to identify closely with someone or something, we come to know another point of view, another way of perceiving the world. This kind of knowing is an essential aspect of creative thinking. While you may not be ready to sit on a nest of eggs, it is not difficult to imagine yourself as a piece of fruit, a butterfly, or another person for a brief period of time.

Developing Awareness Through Experience

To help you understand the relationship of awareness to experience, read and answer the questions below. The subject is strawberries. Check "yes" if you have ever...

Yes	No	
		planted strawberry plants and watched them grow
		devised a way to keep birds and insects from eating them
		picked and washed them
		pulled out the stems
		sliced strawberries
		mashed strawberries
		eaten strawberry shortcake
		served strawberries over ice cream
		added them to fruit salad
		made strawberry jam
		dipped them in powdered sugar before eating them
		photographed a strawberry
		enjoyed a beverage made from strawberries

If more "no" than "yes" responses are recorded, it might be a good idea to try experiencing strawberries in new ways. Select one experience to remember in greater detail. Let's imagine that you have chosen the first experience on the list. By asking some questions about this experience, you can explore and recall it in greater breadth. When you planted the strawberry plant, did you notice the size, weight, and vitality of the plant? Was the ground dry or moist? Did you crumble the dirt in your hands and smell it? Did you uncover any worms or stones as you prepared the soil?

Developing Awareness Through Details

The following list enumerates the details of a strawberry. As you read each item, check the "yes" or "no" column. Have you ever noticed...

Yes	No	
		the shape of a strawberry
		the weight of a strawberry
		the amount of moisture in a strawberry
		how it smells
		the degree of sweetness
		the variation in skin color
		how many seeds are on its skin
		the white tuft lining the inside
		how much hollow space is on the inside
		how it feels to rub the strawberry's skin against your own
		the texture of the skin
		how an over-ripe strawberry tastes

If you checked "yes" on more than half, you are above average in your knowledge of the details of a strawberry.

Developing Awareness Through Empathy

As you think about the items listed below, imagine that you are a strawberry.
Can you feel what it's like to ...

Yes	No	
		have the sun warm you
		get cold at night
		feel rain drop on you
		have someone put their nose in your face and sniff
		feel yourself growing riper and plumper everyday
		have bugs crawl over you
		be picked off the stem
		change from a blossom into a newly formed, green berry
		be washed in the kitchen sink
		be sitting in a bowl with many other strawberries

By thinking about these questions, you have probably gained a better understanding of empathy. If more of these were checked "yes" than "no," you are
definitely on your way to creative thinking. However, if you had more "no"
responses, it would be a good idea to practice identifying with objects so you
can develop this important skill.

who exhibit a high degree of awareness serve as excellent
r students. Such teachers are flexible and fluent in their
their students an ever changing menu of experience and
om. Field trips, the use of multiple forms of media, guest
iagery, and hands-on encounters are an on-going part of
iey vary their teaching methods, often using approaches
students to become more independent in thought and

Many children's books are written with a high degree of sensitivity. They offer unique avenues of sensory exploration. *Hailstones and Halibut Bones* by Mary O'Neil is an excellent book for a teacher to read to children on the perception of color. *Do You Hear What I Hear?* by Helen Borten deals with sounds from those beyond the human range, such as a daisy petal, to the sound of a full symphony orchestra. *Anna Banana And Me*, a beautifully illustrated book by Lenore Blegvad, helps children to bask in the magic of their everyday experiences. Older students will enjoy listening to selected passages from award winning novels such as *Bridge to Terabithia* by Katherine Patterson or *Summer of the Monkeys* by Wilson Rawls. Compile your own personal list of children's books or novels in relation to awareness of experience, details, and empathy. Read aloud these selected books or passages and encourage students to help you locate additional books for this purpose.

Make copies of the three strawberry awareness charts and have your students respond to them. Then ask students to develop their own awareness charts. They may wish to relate them to the geographical location in which you live or a unit of study in the classroom. Students may also want to make similar charts for each of the five senses.

When students have experienced making and sharing their own awareness charts, they may be ready to construct an awareness booklet. In this booklet they write about what awareness means to them. Then they choose a topic to explore—perhaps animals, plant life, people, color, texture, or food. Photographs and drawings about their topic are collected and studied. The best of the visuals are arranged in a pleasing fashion on the pages of the booklet, leaving ample space for students to record their sensory impressions and thoughts. The completed booklet will be a kind of photo-essay that makes a personal statement about the topic.

You can also set aside time each day for students to keep a sensory journal of some object in the environment that they can experience daily. Have them record something new about it each day for a week or perhaps even longer. They can try to look at it from a new point of view or perspective. They might imagine seeing things in it or wonder how it could be modified to make it more attractive, valuable, or fun to play with. How would it look in different surroundings? What other function could it serve?

Some Closing Thoughts

Our understanding of the modes of perception allows us to help students perceive their environment. Since perception is learned, we can and must provide learning tasks to increase our students' perceptual abilities. In doing so, it should be stressed that all three aspects of perceptual awareness need to be brought into play. For it is only when experience, the details of that experience, and empathy or identification are brought together in an aesthetic relationship that a momentary wholeness in the creative process is achieved.

Our awareness goal should be to:

Open ourselves to new experiences and sensory impressions.
Focus on the details of our experiences.
Identify or empathize with the experience of others.
Find new ways "to know" something. An unusual view can be experienced through sound and smell as well as sight.
Immerse ourselves thoroughly in sensory experiences before making any attempt to structure them.

Education for sensory intelligence should become an integral part of every school's curriculum so that students can participate fully in the creative process.

building mental images
for visual thinking

Students in our classrooms are filled with a wealth of experience and ideas. Much of their experience is stored by the brain in inner images. We can help students to draw upon this great inner treasure by introducing them to a process known as imagery, a method used to guide the "inner eye" or "mind's eye" to visualize an object, a situation, or an event. During imagery a person experiences images on a screen inside the head. While focusing on a particular image, the mind automatically slows down to limit the number of distractions. This stilling of the mind enhances the vividness and clarity of the image. When you, as the projectionist, choose to slow down the picture, there is time to examine the elements of the picture in detail. New connections and associations are formed as visual thought is allowed to be active.

Unfortunately, imagery is not often used in the classroom. I believe this is due to the fact that contemporary education affords little if any opportunity for teachers and students to develop this inner resource. Many teachers use imagery in their classrooms on one or two occasions and do not feel comfortable. Perhaps two or three students are noisy and disruptive during the process while others insist that they are unable to see anything at all when their eyes are closed. These kinds of experiences are commonplace when imagery is first introduced. A teacher who is knowledgeable and confident about imagery knows such obstacles will soon disappear if a plan of action is taken. The plan of action which I adopted after working with teachers, many of whom were skeptical about using imagery in their classrooms, consists of the following three steps:

1. Educate yourself about imagery and its usefulness as a tool for learning.

2. Share this information with your students.

3. Guide your students through a series of imagery exercises designed to build their inner vision. (Please refer to the exercises on page 152.)

When I realized that imagery, like reading, is a skill that can be developed, the rest was easy. The exercises are brief and easy to use. Once they are completed, I no longer consider my students to be "in training." I then begin using imagery that will help students become more successful in all subject areas.

Imagery can be used to introduce concepts and ideas in many if not all academic subjects. In history it can be utilized to introduce a new chapter or to provide information about an event such as the Boston Tea Party. During science students enjoy forming images of different cloud formations or following the journey of red blood cells through the circulatory system. When studying fractions, students image different shaped figures and then identify fractional parts of these same figures. Throughout the year I use imagery to help students create fresh ideas for stories and essays. The possibilities are unlimited. Many teachers I know enjoy writing imagery scripts to fit their own needs. However, there are some wonderful books containing numerous examples of imagery that can be used by classroom teachers. Two of my favorites are *200 Ways of Using Imagery in the Classroom* by Michael Bagley and Karin Hess and *Enhancing Writing Through Imagery* by Karin Hess.[22]

I have found that imagery is a very effective method to increase the achievement of cognitive skills in my classroom. Although some of my students need more practice than others to develop this skill, within a few weeks everyone is successfully involved in the process. As a result of using imagery I have observed the following benefits:

- Increased creativity in verbal and written expression
- Increased reading comprehension
- Improved concentration and focusing skills
- Improved memory and retention

Some studies have shown evidence of increased reading comprehension scores when students are able to generate and manipulate visual images of the material being read. When imagery is used to introduce or reinforce the material from a story within the basal reader, students are more responsive in group discussions about the story. They also obtain higher scores on quizzes.

The Three Elements of an Image

The first element of an image is a pictorial one, the visual representation of an object, thing, or event. The vividness and clarity of the image will vary among people but with practice anyone can improve the quality of a visual picture. Visual images can be seen in real life colors. Once a person has identified with a visual image, it is possible to receive a somatic or feeling response. This emotional response may be characterized as joyful, sad, humorous, happy, or perhaps even fearful. The nature and degree of somatic experience depends upon the vividness of the image and the content of the image. The last element of an image is meaning, which is the new understanding about the content of an image. When the visual picture is in focus and evoking some emotional response, the end result is meaning. A complete and successful imagery experience should include all three elements: visual, somatic, and meaning.

Conditions for Imaging

According to Michael Bagley and Karin Hess, authors of *200 Ways of Using Imagery in the Classroom*, there are four major conditions that facilitate imaging.[23] The first condition or step is for the imager to identify with some object, thing, or situation. In this early stage, the student draws upon various concepts in order to formulate an identification with the thing to be imaged. For instance, you might ask students to image themselves climbing a high mountain. Just prior to beginning the image, each student will form or conceptualize a meaning of mountain. This conceptualization process enables the student to form an identification with the construct, mountain. Within seconds, the image of a mountain will follow.

Relaxation, the second and perhaps most important condition, allows the student to experience deep concentration. A tense, anxious mind will impede the natural flow of images. It is true that the imagery process itself can result in a state of relaxation, but it is advisable to start the imagery exercise with some level of relaxation already in operation. Discuss the importance of relaxation with your students so that they too can value its special relationship to imagery. You may even wish to use a short relaxation technique before initiating an imagery exercise.

The next condition is acceptance. Images that appear on each individual's personal screen must not be labeled, evaluated, rejected, or analyzed. Any kind of verbalization automatically knocks the image right off the screen. Some students experience great difficulty as they try to remain open to visualized images. Because they are so highly conditioned to be verbal and analytical, these individuals will need a lot of practice. Children adapt so much more easily to a non-verbal state than adults because they have had less conditioning and formal education.

The final condition for ensuring quality imagery is concentration. After the student has successfully identified with an object, thing, or event, the last goal is to reach a deep level of concentration where all outside distractions are completely removed from conscious awareness so images will develop spontaneously. These images will evoke positive emotional responses and meanings which may appear in the form of new ideas, thoughts, and actions. A student who images life in a fishing village, for example, may gain new emotional perspectives about the village people and their daily involvement in the fishing business.

The ability to concentrate is something students can develop and cultivate. It is a skill anyone can learn. To heighten concentration, teachers can ask students to focus on particular details in an image and then scan the entire image for colors, shapes, and texture. Another method to improve concentration involves having students refocus on the same image 2-3 times. Each time the student repeats any image, s/he will usually see something new, something that was not previously realized.

Imagery Exercises

The following exercises are presented and sequenced according to their complexity. Take time to do these exercises in the order in which they are presented. Students will experience more success in imaging if they are introduced to the process gradually. After each exercise, discuss their reactions to the various experiences. Your students will provide you with important feedback on their progress so you will be able to share their exciting experiences and deal with any difficulty they may have in adjusting to their particular kind of visual learning.

Exercise #1 Seeing a 2-Dimensional Picture
Select a two-dimensional black and white picture similar to the kind found in coloring books. Tell students to look at the picture for 10 seconds. Then have

students close their eyes and see it in their mind's eye for 10 seconds. Discuss what happened. Allow plenty of time for students to share both negative and positive experiences. Have students again look at the picture and concentrate on details for 10-15 seconds. Students then close their eyes and see it in their mind's eye for 30 seconds. Discuss the experience.

Note: Build on this initial experience by introducing two or three other black and white pictures which are more detailed and complex. When students are comfortable imaging black and white pictures, select one or two colored prints for them to image.

Exercise #2 Pencil or Pen
Instruct students to relax and look at any pencil or pen for 15 seconds, studying its detail. Then say:

Relax and close your eyes
See the pencil or pen
Notice its shape
See its color
See its point
Feel the surface with your fingers
When I count to three, open your eyes

Note: Allow approximately 15 seconds for each suggestion.

Exercise #3 An Old Pair of Shoes
Briefly discuss one of your favorite pairs of shoes that were discarded after they became too small or worn and read the following poem:

My Garden Shoes

They look like battle-scarred canoes —
My weather-beaten garden shoes.
They have no fear of morning dew;
We launch right out and wade on through
To garden plots, the barn, the shed;
With toes upturned, we plod ahead.
The heels have long ago gone tilt,
Forgetting how they first were built.

Am I complaining? No siree!
They finally feel so good on me.

Dorothy Gistettenbauer Colgan

Then say:
Close your eyes and relax
Breathe deeply two times
Remember a favorite pair of shoes you used to wear
See these shoes
Notice their shape and contour

See the lines of stitching on the surface
Look at the soles
See yourself walking in these shoes
Notice how your feet feel as your walk
Now see yourself removing these shoes
Notice the places where they are worn or scuffed
When I count to 5, slowly open your eyes

Exercise #4 A Red Apple
Close your eyes and relax
Breathe deeply two times
See a large red apple
Notice its size and shape
Look for any small imperfections on the surface
Hold the apple in your hands and run your fingers over the surface
Feel the weight
Now see yourself taking a bite
Hear the crunch and enjoy the taste
Smell the apple
Look at the whole apple one more time
When I count to three, open your eyes

Exercise #5 A Feather
If possible, give each student a feather to explore before this exercise begins.

Find a comfortable position
Close your eyes and breathe deeply two times
See your feather
Notice every line and edge of it... the tip... and the fluff around the quill
Pick up your feather and brush it across the back of your hand... across your
   arm...
Notice how it feels
Now imagine that you are your feather
You are sitting on a table, next to an open window
A gust of wind lifts you and carries you out the window
High above the houses, over the trees and far up into the sky
Look down and see the entire city
You are floating... twisting... dipping and gliding
Feel the warmth of the sun
The wind has stopped
You are drifting slowly downward... down... down
A gentle breeze carries you back through the window and onto the table
   where you first began this adventure
Your journey has ended
Open your eyes when I count to ten

Exercise #6 Your Grandmother or Grandfather
Close your eyes
Sit comfortably and breathe deeply two times
Picture your grandmother sitting across from you
Look at her face
Notice the shape and color of her eyes

See the skin
Notice the texture and color of her face
Now see the expression on her face
Listen to your grandmother speak
See your grandmother doing something she often does
Notice the clothing she wears
Once again, see her face
When I count to 10, open your eyes

Exercise #7 Yourself
Sit comfortably and relax
Close your eyes
Breathe deeply two times
See yourself standing in a room
Notice your face
See the color of your eyes and hair
Study the contour of your nose, cheeks, and jaw
See your whole body
Notice the clothes you are wearing
See yourself talking to someone
Listen to your voice as you speak
Again see your face
When I count to 10, slowly open your eyes

When your students have completed these seven exercises, they will be ready to participate in imagery which can be used in any subject area. The following imagery is used to introduce an art activity. As you create your own imagery exercises, keep your statements simple and avoid asking questions. Use words such as feel, notice, look, etc., to start each suggestion. Present each suggestion very slowly and naturally. Below is an example of an imagery exercise to introduce an art activity.

Pattern Designs

Art Activity:
    Students will experiment with different shapes and colors of construction paper to create a pattern design.

Imagery Exercise:
    Sit comfortably and relax
    See yourself in front of a large computer
    Program a shape to appear on the wide video screen
    See the shape
    Notice its color
    Change its color
    Fill the space with more of these shapes
    Move them around... take some away... let them overlap
    Enlarge some
    Add a new shape
    Make lots of them
    See all the shapes mix
    Watch as a pattern of colors and shapes begins to form
    See yourself returning to the classroom
    When I count to ten, open your eyes

art appreciation

Students taking an art appreciation course for the first time often ask, "What should I be looking for?" Such a question suggests that there is something hidden in a work of art separate from the work itself, something that can be communicated with a verbal description. It stems from the deep-seated belief that whatever seems vague and confusing in the visual realm can be fully clarified by translation into words. This is not so. If a work of art has value, it is whole and complete in and of itself. It may imply many things beyond itself, but these things are usually details of a peripheral nature. The message to the viewer is in the work of art itself.

What is it that prevents so many of us from relating to pictures as works of art? I am convinced that it has to do with the division of pictures into two categories: informational and emotional. Generally speaking, informational pictures are used to illustrate other ideas, things which are possible to see and describe in words. Pictures of this kind are easily understood by everyone. In fact, they are not usually seen as pictures at all, but as substitutes for the objects portrayed. Informational pictures have a definite factual value, but we need to learn how to value the emotional qualities found in other kinds of pictures.

Attending to What We See in Art

There are two ways to draw attention to a work of art you are going to experience: the first is to identify the work; the second is to describe it. To identify a work of art in a scholarly manner, students should know:

1. The title of the work
2. The artist who made it
3. The date when it was created
4. The place where it was made
5. The medium or materials from which it was made

Knowing the country an artist lived in or the period in which he worked can give students some clues about the original purpose or use of the art object. Nevertheless, students will probably be most interested in the present meaning and purpose of a work of art. They will want to know how it affects their lives and world outlook right now. For this reason, many teachers prefer to emphasize describing, rather than identifying a work of art, because it immediately involves students in using their eyes and minds to understand what they are looking at.

The following critical process for looking at and describing works of art can be used for students at the elementary level as well as older students. The critical process consists of the following three stages:

1. Describe the subject matter and the elements and principles of art
2. Analyze the elements and principles of art
3. Interpret the art work

It is probably a good idea to embark on stage 1, describing the subject matter and the art elements, after students have completed the five steps in identifying a work of art. When a "positive identification" has been completed, have students describe the subject of the painting or other work. Discuss all literal aspects such as the presence of animals, people, fruit, trees, objects, atmosphere, and all of the qualities which generate the impression of reality or abstraction. In addition, take time to consider whether the work is based on an event in history, mythology, or an invention of the artist's imagination.

When the subject has been thoroughly explored, move into a discussion of the artist's use of line, shape, color, and texture. Talk about the kind of lines used, the variety of shapes, the value and intensity of color, and the use of implied texture. When you discuss line, keep in mind the following characteristics of line direction:

The vertical line appears as standing and can give an impression of formality and poise. There is often a connection between vertical lines and virtue. Church steeples reach skyward and a respected man is sometimes described as "upright."

A horizontal line appears as lying down. It has a feeling of rest and inaction and provides a ground plane for vertical lines. Represented by a horizontal line, the horizon always seems peaceful and elicits a quiet, restful feeling.

The diagonal is off balance. For this reason, not many paintings are based on the diagonal alone. A strong diagonal acts as a counterbalance to the picture.

A curve is a rhythmic, moving line. Paintings based on curving lines are apt to contain many other related curves. Gaiety, movement, and action are often expressed in related curving lines.

All pictures are a combination of many directional lines, some dominant and others subordinated.

In the first stage students describe what they see. In stage two, students are required to go one step further as they analyze the relationships among the things they see. It is time to discover how shapes affect or influence each other. Order, balance, proportion, contrast, rhythm, and color relationships are among the several principles of art used by artists to create a composition.

Imagine two circles side by side and two other identical circles, one above the other. Although the shapes are the same in each example, their relationships are different. The first set is horizontal while the other set is vertical. Obviously, each of these shape relationships has a different effect on the viewer. The way shapes are arranged, then, is an important consideration in understanding a work of art.

What do we know about the principle of balance? First, a feeling for balance is instinctive. A child struggles to keep her balance when she is first learning to skate. Few of us can resist the impulse to move a lamp to the center of the table if it stands too near the edge. In fact, any piece of furniture slightly off-angle from the wall is highly visible and demands our attention. It is this kind of instinct that underlies and unifies pictorial composition. In the diagram below, notice how the odd, the out-of-relation square, is immediately apparent in both cases.

Size relationships need to be considered. We do not see shapes or objects in isolation. We see them in pairs, clusters, or groups. Particular attention is given to the largest or smallest shape. We also notice when the size is about the same. In any event, proportion is significant because it gives us clues about importance. (Large shapes usually seem more important.) Also size provides a clue about location in space when you are looking at a picture in which spatial depth is represented.

Color mixing is a science that is predictable and can be formulated. However, the use of color in painting is considered an art. In works of art, colors are creative tools, used for their emotional effect rather than as parts of "color schemes."

For the painter, color primarily consists of two factors: complementaries and the opposition of warm to cold. Both properties are displayed in the diagram below. This diagram is based on pigments rather than on the primaries of light. A mixture of the three pigment primaries — red, yellow, and blue — will produce any known color. A mixture of equal amounts of any two primary colors will become the complement of the third primary color. Adjacent complementary colors on the color wheel will accent one another and, since they both appear brighter, they have the effect of extending the available color range.

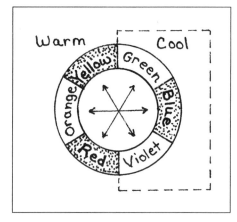

Warm and cool colors also accent one another but to a lesser degree. Their most noticeable effect is in the creation of volume and space. The color wheel is divided into warm colors on the left and cold on the right. However, this should be interpreted loosely, for warm and cold are not absolute, but relative. Certain reds, for example, appear warm in isolation but will appear cool against a warmer red. Remember that colors are affected by texture, size, and shape. Have students notice whether the colors of related shapes are similar or different from each other, whether they vary slightly or contrast strongly. Talk about the value relationship — whether a color area is lighter or darker than a nearby area. Sometimes the colors are different while the values are the same. These

Post a color wheel in a prominent place so it can be used for reference as you study the colors in a work of art.

kinds of observations may be useful later on when you try to interpret the entire work of art.

Texture and surface relationships add a wonderful dimension to our lives. For example, when you walk into a bakery to buy an assortment of cookies, you can usually tell, as you look through the glass window, which cookies are soft and cake-like, which are chewy, and which ones will be brittle and crunchy. When you go out on a rainy day, it is easy to observe how rain alters the surface of sidewalks, streets, grass, and the atmosphere that surrounds us. You can often tell whether a piece of metal is dirty or clean, new or old, or even whether it is hot or cold. We need to make these same observations when studying a piece of art. For it is this type of observation that helps us discover the emotional qualities as well as the ideas conveyed by the art object.

During stage 3, the interpretation of a work of art, you decide what all your earlier observations mean. A critical interpretation, a statement about a work of art, enables the visual observations to fit together and make sense. It is an idea or concept that seems to summarize and unify all of the individual traits of the painting or art object. Realize that an interpretation does not describe the object. Nor does it try to translate visual qualities into verbal language. This has already been accomplished in previous stages. Words are now used to describe ideas, ideas that serve to clarify the sensations and feelings we have in the presence of the art object. An interpretation might also be regarded as an explanation of a work of art.

In stating what the goal or aim of the work of art is, we are not necessarily saying what the artist's purpose was. It is unlikely that we really know the intent of the artist. As critics, it is our job to state only what the visual evidence seems to suggest, regardless of the artist's aims. Sometimes an artist's statement about his work is helpful in suggesting good places to look for visual information. Nevertheless, an important rule of art criticism is: Base your interpretation on what you have seen and felt in the work, not on what someone has said about it.

When students are interpreting a particular painting, you may want to ask them to participate in one or more of the following activities:

1. Divide the class into small groups. Ask each group to create their own title for the painting. Make a list of all the suggested titles on a piece of chart paper and discuss them.

2. Discuss how music and art are related. Then play three different pieces of music. Ask students to select the piece of music they believe best interprets the painting in question. Each student must provide a rationale for her/his choice.

3. Hold a class discussion about where to hang a particular piece of art. A student may suggest hanging it in a bedroom, the kitchen, or perhaps in the main hall of a stately old castle. Whatever the suggestion, a student must give a reason for deciding on a particular location.

Creating an Art Appreciation Program for Your Classroom or School

Teachers who want to create a curriculum for art appreciation in their classroom or school often feel overwhelmed. The subject matter is so expansive that it is sometimes difficult to know where to begin. Fortunately, you don't have to be an expert art critic or historian to teach your students about the priceless value of our art heritage. Some suggestions for creating an art appreciation program for your students include:

1. Any subject can be expanded to include relevant art work. For example, art prints and objects can be found which incorporate mathematical concepts like symmetry, shape, geometric form, and pattern. In social studies, art can be found which reflects the architecture, customs, folklore, history, and heroes of a particular time and place. Brainstorm subject areas and search out art examples to fit your needs.

2. Many teachers emphasize the elements and principles of art during weekly art periods. When you are focusing on one of the art elements, such as color, collect and display a series of art prints which portray this particular element. Looking, talking, and evaluating can be done before or after a hands-on activity. The skills developed through these "appreciation sessions" will help students to evaluate their own work.

3. A theme study organizes artwork by subject or categories. This system works well in a self-contained classroom or an art room setting. Typical examples include:

-still lifes	-children	-animals
-portraits	-families	-horses
-landscapes	-famous people	-cats
-make-believe	-ordinary people	-dogs

Research has indicated that elementary age children prefer realism, bright colors, and familiar subject matter. When making selections to discuss with your class, keep these points in mind but do not limit your selections to those works that have only these characteristics. Also select examples that you feel positive about because your interest can make the difference. Use large, clear examples that your class can view easily and keep in mind that several examples are better than just one. For example, three Van Gogh prints will illustrate his unique style better than one. Also a comparison between a work that illustrates a concept and a work that does not will make the ideas clearer to the students.

At Washington Elementary School in Visalia, California, a committee of teachers planned an art appreciation program for their school. They decided to select a group of four artists to study at each level. Each group is composed of one American and one European artist and is representative of impressionistic, realistic, and abstract art. Fortunately, teachers are able to check out the art prints they will use from the District Media Center. The committee has prepared a biographical sketch of each artist for teachers to use in their art discussions. Teachers are pleased with the program. As they share art with their students, new insights are gained from the curious and unique perspective that looking and talking about art with the young provides.

Before you present an art appreciation lesson, read as much as you can about your subject. The adult and children's section of most city and/or school district libraries hold a variety of excellent materials. Become familiar with magazines which feature articles about art, works of art, or artists. You can build your own collection of prints from *School Arts, Arts and Activities*, and the covers of *Instructor* magazine. Museum shops sell prints, postcard reproductions, slides, and booklets. In fact, some museums have educational divisions especially formed to work with teachers and school children. The National Gallery of Art in Washington, D.C. sends free of charge many slide sets and other visual materials to schools. Write to their extension service at the following address for information: National Gallery of Art, Washington, D.C. 20565. And whenever possible, visit an artist's studio, a nearby gallery, or the nearest university's art department. As wonderful as prints, slides, and films can be, there is nothing like the real thing. ✐

in conclusion ...

On Thursday afternoon the music teacher routinely takes my class. During this weekly lesson, I direct my attention to planning or grading. However, one afternoon I became one of her students as she introduced "Peter and the Wolf" to the class. First she read the story aloud. Then we all listened to the entire piece of music. Although I had a large stack of papers to grade by the following day, it was impossible to turn away from the lilting notes of the flute and the deep drama of the drums.

The following week our beloved music teacher returned and the students reviewed the previous week's lesson. Then they were asked to draw their own interpretation of one episode from "Peter and the Wolf." I knew that this would be an enjoyable assignment for this fourth grade class because their drawing skills were superior. Even so, I was amazed by the rich detail and energy which flowed across their papers. The drawings were magnificent, primarily because they conveyed so much about each student's understanding of this musical drama. At the end of the period, the teacher told students how much she admired their drawings. Then she announced that it would not be necessary for them to take a quiz on "Peter and the Wolf" because she had already given everyone an A. My students were elated but also quite surprised. They wanted to know why. The teacher simply said, "Your wonderful drawings show me that you have learned everything I want you to know about 'Peter and the Wolf'. Giving you a quiz now would simply be a waste of everyone's time. In fact, a quiz could not possibly convey as much information as your drawings have."

What a significant moment for all of us! Several students turned around to see if Mrs. Mason had been "tuned in" to the music teacher's final words. My broad smile and incredible joy soon answered their question. We had been pursuing this business of visual thinking for a long time. Now "someone else" recognized and appreciated our developing skills. What a wonderful gift she had given us.

When we provide students with a curriculum that emphasizes visual as well as verbal thinking skills, they become more observant of everything in their environment. This increased visual awareness enables them to create a bountiful storehouse of inner images that can be retrieved instantly. In my experience, students read with better comprehension when they are able to form mental images of the printed word. Their original stories and poems are more detailed and creative if ideas are visualized beforehand. But most important, students who are visual thinkers have a powerful method for generating new ideas and possibilities whenever any challenge arises. Their inner screens fill with images that they will find a way to express.

As you may have gathered from the first page of this book, I was not born a gifted visual thinker. The work I do with my students has enabled me to develop this much needed skill. Because I sometimes sketch an old shoe or a small flower, I'm beginning to see many things I've never noticed before. These images and countless others find their way into the library of my inner world every day. They supply the creative force that enables me to imagine my daily life into something more beautiful and enjoyable. One day I found myself visualizing *Beyond Words*. It never occurred to me that I would one day be an author. However, the detailed images that continued to form in my mind made it impossible for me not to write this book.

I would love to see every teacher create a visual thinking curriculum for students. The benefits of such a curriculum are "plainly visible" every single day. Furthermore, I know that those who do will receive many personal as well professional rewards as they journey *Beyond Words*.

end notes

1. McKim, Robert. *Experiences in Visual Thinking.* Boston, Massachusetts: PWS Engineering, 1980. p. 29.

2. Ibid., p. 10.

3. Einstein, A., quoted by Hadamard, J. *The Psychology of Invention in the Mathematical Field.* Princeton University Press.

4. McKim, p. 8.

5. Lanier, Vincent. *The Arts We See.* New York: Teachers College Press, 1982, p. 26.

6. Feldman, Edmund. *Becoming Human Through Art.* Englewood Cliffs, New Jersey: Prentice-Hall, Inc., 1970, p. 16.

7. Arnheim, Rudolf. *Visual Thinking.* Los Angeles: University of California Press, 1969.

8. Ibid. p. 295.

9. Koestler, Arthur: *The Act of Creation.* MacMillan.

10. Edwards, Betty. *Drawing On The Artist Within.* Simon and Schuster, New York, 1986, p. 66.

11. *"Creating A Legend."* Art and Man. Published by Scholastic, Inc. under the direction of the National Gallery of Art, p. 11.

12. Edwards

13. Edwards, p. 50.

14. McKim, p. 68.

15. Unsworth, Jean. *"Connecting Through the Arts: From the Inside Out."* School Arts. Volume 85, No. 6, Worchester, Massachusetts: Davis Publications, p. 18.

16. Prebble, Duanne. *Art Creates Man Creates Art.* Berkeley, California: McCuthan Publishing Corporation, 1973, p. 12.

17. Linderman, E. and Herberholz D. *Developing Artistic and Perceptual Awareness.* William C. Brown Publishers, 1977, p. 18.

18. Linderman, p. 20.

19. Edwards, pgs. 3 - 4.

20. Linderman, p. 23.

21. Brittain, W. and Lowenfeld, V. *Creative and Mental Growth*. New York: MacMillan, 1975.

22. Bagley, Michael and Hess, Karen. *200 Ways of Using Imagery in the Classroom: A Guide for Developing the Imagination and Creativity of Elementary and Intermediate Students*. New York, New York: Trillium Press, 1984.

23. Bagley, p. 8.

bibliography

Arnheim, Rudolf. *Visual Thinking*. Los Angeles: University of California Press, 1969.

Bagley, Michael and Karen Hess. *200 Ways of Using Imagery in the Classroom: A Guide for Developing the Imagination and Creativity of Elementary and Intermediate Students.* New York, New York: Trillium Press, 1984.

Brethers, Ray. *The Language of Paintings: Form and Content*. New York: Atman Publishing Corporation, 1963.

Brittain, W. and Lowenfeld, V. *Creative and Mental Growth*. New York: Macmillan, 1975.

Brookes, Mona. *Drawing With Children*. Los Angeles, California: S.P. Tarcher, Inc. 1986.

Brown, Lauann Brown. *Art Appreciation for the Popsicle Generation*. Carthage, Illinois: Good Apple, Inc., 1984.

"Creating A Legend." Art and Man. Published by Scholastic, Inc. under the direction of the National Gallery of Art.

Edwards, Betty. *Drawing on the Right Side of the Brain*. J.P. Tarcher, Los Angeles, California: Distributed by St. Martin's Press, N.Y., 1979.

Edwards, Betty. *Drawing on the Artist Within*. New York: Simon and Schuster, 1986.

Eisner, Elliot. *Cognition and Curriculum: A Basis For Deciding What To Teach*. New York: Longman, 1982.

Feldman, Edmund. *Becoming Human Through Art*. Englewood Cliffs, New Jersey: Prentice-Hall, 1970.

Koestler, Arthur. *The Act of Creation*. Macmillan.

Lanier, Vincent. *The Arts We See*. New York: Teachers College Press, 1982.

Linderman, E. and D. Herberholz. *Developing Artistic and Perceptual Awareness*. William C. Brown Publishers, 1977.

McCarthy, Bernice. *The 4MAT System: Teaching To Learning Styles with Right/Left Mode Techniques*. Barrington, Illinois: Excel, Inc., 1980, 1988.

McCarthy, Bernice and Susan Leflar. *4MAT in Action*. Excel, Inc., 1983.

Powell, William. *The World of Color and How To Use It*. Tustin, California: A Walter Foster Publication, 1984.

Prebble, Duanne. *Art Creates Man Creates Art*. Berkeley, California: McCuthan Publishing Corporation, 1973.

Unsworth, Jean. *"Connecting Through The Arts: From the Inside Out."* School Arts. Volume 85, No. 6, Worchester, Massachusetts: Davis Publications, P. 18.

Zdenek, Marilee. *The Right Brain Experience*. New York: McGraw-Hill Book Company, 1983.